Total Capitalism

Market Politics, Market State

Colin Leys

MERLIN PRESS

© Colin Leys, 2008

First published 2008 by Three Essays Collective, India

First UK edition published 2008 by
The Merlin Press
96 Monnow Street
Monmouth
NP25 3EQ
Wales

www.merlinpress.co.uk

ISBN. 9780850365900

British Library Cataloguing in Publication Data
is available from the British Library

Printed in the UK by Lightning Source, Milton Keynes

Total Capitalism

CONTENTS

INTRODUCTION

I recently received a circular from the Local Authority of the district in London where I live, which addressed me as a 'customer'. I should really be inured by now to neoliberalism's relentless penetration of the 'life world', but it took me aback all the same. I don't buy anything from my local council; on the contrary, it is supposed to represent me. I elect it, and it spends my taxes. But in the mind of the official who wrote the circular it is evidently more like a corporation with something to sell: satisfaction, perhaps.

The example is trivial, but sobering all the same. The dream of contemporary capitalism is that everything should become a terrain of profitable enterprise, including most of what has hitherto been seen as the business of government. The political rationale offered for this is that in a globalized world national competitiveness depends on maximising efficiency, including the efficiency of public services, and that competition between market actors makes for efficiency. The local government official who had learned to think of electors not as sovereign citizens but as customers was merely reflecting this doctrine. But I was struck by an analogy: the vision of society implied by seeing citizens as customers – a society totally dedicated to capitalism – is not unlike the concept of 'total war' developed in the early years of the first World War – 'a war fought…between entire societies and not just between armies'.[1]

Of course the organisational principle of total war is different in a crucial respect from that of the total capitalism advocated by neoliberals today. Under total war, 'in all the belligerent nations, to a greater or lesser degree, civil and economic liberties, the free market, even national sovereignty, gave way to a kind of military socialism', with a proliferation of state agencies and controls. Under total capitalism, by contrast, the free market is the supreme value to which not just national sovereignty and civil liberties, but all public and private life, are increasingly subordinated – to the point where the distinction between public and private functions increasingly as a useful fiction. Public transport, education, health care, social services, scientific research, telecommunications, broadcasting, publishing, pensions, foreign aid, land use, water, the public infrastructure, the arts, and public policy-making itself, are increasingly entrusted to private sector personnel seconded into government ministries: all become subject to market-driven policy-making in the name of 'efficiency', and are treated more and more as fields for profitable private investment rather than as means to a better society.

The three essays in this book are about the arrival and implications of total capitalism, and span a decade of work. The first, 'The Rise and Fall of Development Theory', is taken from a book of the same title published in 1996, which summed up my thoughts on what had happened to the field in which I had worked for most of my life. It is about theory, but it is not a work of theory: it is really about the material world in which a collective project called 'development' could be the subject of a theory, and about how the triumph of neoliberal globalisation put an end to both project and theory.

The second essay is largely drawn from the first part of my book, *Market-Driven Politics*, published in 2001. In it I tried to analyse the determining features of the new politics. It seemed to me that with the end of capital controls, the politics of most once-sovereign states would be bound to become much more dependent on market forces, and on the politics of economic superpowers, as the politics of small 'third world' countries had always been, with profoundly negative implications for democracy. I chose to study Britain because it was my home country (although I had lived elsewhere for most of my working life), and because under Mrs Thatcher it had taken a lead in the world-wide abandonment of social democracy in favour of total capitalism; but I think that the analysis is of quite general application, and has stood the test of time.

In order to overcome resistance to my argument – a resistance that has weakened, but by no means disappeared, in the years since – I decided to ground it empirically in two closely-analysed fields of public service: public service television, and the National Health Service. The aim was to show in detail how the evolution of policy in these areas reflected less and less an overriding conception of the public interest, and more and more the pressure of newly-liberated global market forces. How far I succeeded, readers of the book must judge for themselves. But some readers tended to see broadcasting and health as what the book was mainly about, rather than test-beds for its more general argument. So I am very glad to have the opportunity to make the general argument stand out independently in the essay presented here.

The third essay, 'The Cynical State', first published in 2005, is really a spin-off from the second: it analyses what happens to policy-making and the quality of public debate under total capitalism. Its thesis also seems to apply more or less everywhere, as the dynamics of total capitalism gather strength.

I hope readers will find the argument persuasive; better still, I hope it will alarm them, even more than they are likely to be alarmed already, and prompt them to engage themselves even more actively in trying at least to expel capitalism from those spheres where it does not belong, and to help in the development of a new non-capitalist principle of social organisation for the future.

But in case the level of alarm aroused by these essays is still not quite enough, let me add a few words about a part of the argument that has been omitted, for reasons of space, from the essay on 'neoliberal democracy' published here: the part about public services. The privatisation of public services is a cardinal element of total capitalism, which has been accepted (sometimes reluctantly, but all too often with a sort of born-again enthusiasm) by many politicians who consider themselves progressive. But when any public service is privatised a lethal dynamic is set in motion – lethal, that is, to social solidarity and the basic equality of citizens on both of which democracy ultimately depends – a dynamic which few politicians seem to understand (saying things like 'it doesn't matter who provides the service, so long as it is paid for out of taxes', etc.).

For a public service to be transformed into a market, several requirements need to be met. First, the service must be reconfigured into a series of discrete elements that can be priced and sold – in a word, it must be transformed into a set of commodities. Instead of hospital care we have hundreds of treatments, or 'finished consultant episodes', all priced according to their varying costs, and billed for. Second, people must be induced to want to buy the service out of their own pockets, normally by cutting the funding for non-market provision, so that its quality and accessibility decline until people are ready to pay for a market-provided alternative. Third, the workforce involved in providing the service must be transformed from one working for collective aims, with a public service ethic, to one working to produce profits for owners of capital, and subject to market discipline (typically involving less job security and more hierarchy).*

---

* A fourth key requirement, that the risk involved is underwritten by the state, at great public expense, is omitted here for the sake of brevity and in order to focus on the key dynamic involved, i.e. the transformation of services under the logic of competitive capital accumulation. It is more fully discussed in *Market-Driven Politics*.

Once the process of commodification is under way a further dynamic comes into operation – the transformation of the newly-commodified services under the pressure of competition. Competitive production always involves 'Taylorism' – the substitution of cheaper labour for more expensive – and standardisation of the product, in the search for scale economies. But past a certain point, services – especially all personal services, or the personal aspect of any service, such as that provided by shop-floor or counter staff – cannot generate the kind of profits that capital can earn from mass-producing material goods, and capital cannot remain in any field which returns much less than the average rate of profit; so the ultimate logic of commodification is to replace the sale of services by the sale of mass-produced material goods, and to transfer to the consumer as much as possible of whatever 'consumption work' is still left over from the service that was formerly provided.[2] Furniture is re-designed so that it can be collected and assembled by the consumer, automatic machines replace bank tellers, computers and email accounts replace postal services, drugs and heart monitors replace nurses, check-out machines replace supermarket check-out staff and check-in machines replace airport check-in staff; there are hotels without staff, lessons without teachers, publishing houses without editors. In every case the production and consumption process is redesigned so that whatever work can't be done mechanically is done by the consumer.

But this process radically changes the nature of services – in some cases abolishing them entirely – and public services are no exception. A consultation with a family doctor is replaced, first by a consultation with one of a changing team of doctors, and then (when a more profitable 'skill mix' has been installed) by a consultation with a nurse or a nurse-assistant, and finally by a phone call to a medical call-centre, where someone responds following a computerised protocol.

This involves an obvious loss, and so public services then develop in the direction of private services, i.e. with different grades of quality and accessibility, priced according to the respective cost of each level of service provided. You can still get a 'full service' service, but only if you can afford it. This is achieved initially through the introduction of fees for 'extras' of various kinds, but before long these extras come to include things like school books and tuition, decent hospital food, high-quality television programmes, etc., that were originally part of the standard service provided to everybody. What remains available to those without money for extras becomes a highly standardised, residual ('basic') service – or it disappears entirely as a public service, and joins the mass of other private services, in which even the lowest quality must be paid for.

So what began as a public service designed to fulfil a collectively-determined social or political purpose ends up as a drive to find mass-produced goods that can be sold profitably, while the public is differentiated into a hierarchy of individuals, now as unequal in this respect as they are in most others. The collective needs and universal values which the service was originally created to serve are gradually marginalised and finally abandoned. Total capitalism seeks a totally individualised population, without collective needs or universal values; for total capitalism there is, as Mrs Thatcher put it, 'no such thing as society, only individuals and their families', spending their money in markets.

But can we have democracy without society – without a modicum of equality of status and condition, secured by universal public services, and a significant degree of social solidarity based on this? It seems unlikely. And can democracy survive meaningfully when the functions of the state – including its policy-making function, as the last essay in this book shows – are in effect assumed by enormous corporations, run by a small elite of enormously rich people whose supreme principle is maximising 'shareholder value' (including their own share options)? Worse still, is it likely that politicians in such a situation will rise to the challenge of the looming world-wide ecological crisis, when this is driven by capitalism's dependence on indefinitely expanding consumption? Can anyone really believe it? Yet this is where total capitalism is taking us, as fast as we allow it to do so.

I am grateful to James Currey Publisher for permission to include the first essay from *The Rise and Fall of Development Theory* (Oxford: 1996); to Verso for permission to include in the second essay extensive material from *Market-Driven Politics: Neoliberal Democracy and the Public Interest* (London: 2001); and to The Merlin Press for permission to include the third essay from *Telling the Truth: The Socialist Register 2006* (London: 2005). I would also like especially to thank Barbara Harriss-White for the initiative which led to this book, and for constant help and encouragement with it, as with so much else.

The book is dedicated to the memory of W.J.M. (Bill) Mackenzie, an extraordinarily generous mentor and a lifelong intellectual and moral influence.

Notes

1 Encyclopaedia Britannica online: http://www.britannica.com/eb/article-32826

2 The phrase is taken from Ursula Huws' pioneering work on this subject, in *The Making of a Cybertariat* (New York: Monthly Review Press, 2003), citing Batya Weinbaum and Amy Bridges, 'The Other Side of the Paycheck', *Monthly Review*, July-August 1976.

THE RISE & FALL OF DEVELOPMENT THEORY

> To say one more word about preaching what the world ought to be like, philosophy arrives always too late for that. As thought of the world it appears at a time when actuality has completed its developmental process and is finished... When philosophy paints its gray in gray, a form of life has become old, and this gray in gray cannot rejuvenate it, only understand it. The owl of Minerva begins its flight when dusk is falling. (Hegel)[1]

> Only with this universal development of productive forces is a universal intercourse between men established, which produces in all nations simultaneously the phenomenon of the 'propertyless' mass (universal competition) and makes each nation dependent on the revolutions of the others, and finally has put world historical, empirically universal individuals in place of local ones ... How otherwise ... does it happen that trade ... rules the whole world through the relation of supply and demand – a relation which, as an English economist says, hovers over the earth like the fate of the ancients, and with invisible hand allots fortune and misfortune to men, sets up empires and overthrows empires, causes nations to rise and to disappear... (Marx)[2]

As the dusk gradually fell on the twentieth century, the owl of Minerva had a lot on its agenda; with so many illusions to clear up, those for which 'development theory' is responsible might be thought to have had a rather low priority. Yet what is at stake is – or rather was, since the practical ambitions of 'development theory' have been progressively reduced over the years – nothing less than whether human beings can act, collectively, to improve their lot, or whether they must once again accept that it is ineluctably determined by forces – nowadays 'world market forces' – over which they have, in general, little or no control (and least of all those who need it most). Unfortunately, in spite of the importance of the question, 'development theory' has returned only partial and conflicting answers to it.

The first theories of development

To see why, it is useful to begin with an owl's eye view of human history over the past 10,000 years or so since settled agriculture first began to replace hunting and gathering. Agriculture required, but also made possible, an increased specialization of labour, and the development of state apparatuses capable of organizing the defence of cultivated land against outside aggressors and of assuring stability in the increasingly complex social and economic relations on which an agricultural society gradually came to depend. With the establishment of agriculture, then, the process of social evolution greatly accelerated relative to that which had occurred during the preceding 1.8 million years of human life on earth; but for a long time (we may suppose) the process was still sufficiently gradual, and sufficiently precarious at any given place and time, for it not to be felt as an acceleration by the people living through it.

The advent of capitalism in the fifteenth and sixteenth centuries, however, and above all the advent of industrial capitalism in the late eighteenth century, forced the fact of human economic, social, political and cultural development on people's attention. Various thinkers, from Condorcet to Kant, began to conceive of a 'universal history' which would disclose the cumulative pattern and meaning of it all, and its ultimate destination;[3] but the decisive innovators were, of course, Hegel and Marx. Hegel saw world history as a process of development, 'a progression to the better'; but since in his view world history took place 'in the field of the spirit' this progression was only an 'actualization' of the evolving self-understanding of the 'world spirit', in which partial conceptions of the idea of freedom were successively superseded by more and more complete conceptions, through a dialectical process of contradictions and their transcendence.[4] Marx at first followed Hegel, but then jettisoned his metaphysics while retaining the idea of history as progress, seeing it instead as a series of modes of production, each disclosing a higher level than before of the uniquely human capacity for self-realization, and succeeding each other through the working out of contradictions in their inner dynamics.

What makes Hegel and Marx true originators of development theory is that they recognized that it was the sudden acceleration in the rate of change that the establishment of capitalist production and bourgeois society had generated which made it possible and necessary to think of history in this way. Bourgeois society had to be understood historically if it was to be made rational (Hegel's idea), or superseded (Marx's); but this understanding, they both realized, in which capitalist society was seen as the outcome of an evolutionary process stretching back into the mists of time, should also make possible an adequate understanding of earlier societies. As Marx put it, 'Human anatomy is the key to the anatomy of the ape.'[5] Between them they inspired a vast subsequent output of theory-oriented historiography and historically-based social science concerned with understanding the evolution of human life on earth as a structured totality.

The emergence of 'development theory'

But this tradition of thought about development is not what most people have meant by the term 'development theory', which emerged in the 1950s to deal with a far narrower issue: namely, how the economies of the colonies of Britain, France, Portugal and other European powers, colonies comprising some 28% of the world's population, might be transformed and made more productive as decolonization approached, in the context of the still 'semi-colonial' condition of the former colonies of Latin America (accounting for a further 7%).* Understanding this unprecedented event, and gearing policy to these aims, unquestionably called for new theoretical work. But it is striking how little of this work drew on, or even related itself to, the existing body of theory about development that had been prompted by the original advent of capitalism itself.

There were three main reasons for this. First of all, the new 'development theory' had a very strong practical orientation: its aim was to provide grounds for immediate action. Even academic theorists – as opposed to those directly working for development agencies of one sort or another – were drawn to the field by a desire to do something for the peoples of the ex-colonies, and had an even higher degree of conscious commitment to intervention than is usual in most other branches of social science. This militated against philosophical dispassion and reflective self-criticism.

Secondly, the 'new nations' were a prime stake in the Cold War, so that theories of their development were unavoidably contaminated by this. Of course, most development theorists saw their work as science, not propaganda: few were interested in following the example of W.W. Rostow by subtitling any of their works 'A Non-Communist Manifesto'.[6]

But whereas the early theorists of rising capitalism thought it essential to locate it in a broad conception of history, most Western theorists of development in the post-war years (and most of them were Westerners) avoided doing so, because it meant, unavoidably, taking seriously the work of Marx, which at the height of the Cold War was not merely considered unscientific, but in the USA could easily cost you your job.** As a result 'development studies' tended

---

*Estimated from data in Colin McEvedy and Richard Jones, *Atlas of World Population History* (New York: Facts on File, 1978). Fifty years later, population growth had produced a situation where the 'developing countries' (including China) accounted for almost four-fifths of the world's population.

** The degree to which critical social science was systematically rooted out in the USA from 1948 onwards is apt to be forgotten, both by Americans, for whom its consequences have come to be taken as natural, and by foreigners who never experienced it. The consensus of historians is painfully clear that not only did

to be conducted, at least until the mid-1960s, as if they had no significant historical or philosophical roots or presuppositions; and while 'development theorists' were usually glad to affirm their strong normative reasons for being concerned with development, they rarely acknowledged the extent to which their thinking reflected their own political commitments.*

A third crucial conditioning factor in the birth of 'development theory' was the Bretton Woods financial and trading regime. These arrangements were designed to permit national governments to manage their economies so as to maximize growth and employment. Capital was not allowed to cross frontiers without government approval, which permitted governments to determine domestic interest rates, fix the exchange rate of the national currency, and tax and spend as they saw fit to secure national economic objectives. National economic planning was seen as a natural extension of this thinking, as were domestic and international arrangements to stabilize commodity prices. It is not a great oversimplification

---

several hundred university and college professors and high school teachers lose their jobs, while many more were prevented from getting appointments, because of their political views (real or just alleged); but also the complicity of most academic administrators, the systematic use of informers and the weakness of the Association of American University Professors (AAUP) combined with the general jingoism of the time to eliminate virtually any teaching or research that questioned American state policy; 'open criticism of the political status quo disappeared... teachers played it safe, pruning their syllabi and avoiding controversial topics... The academy's enforcement of McCarthyism... silenced an entire generation of radical intellectuals and snuffed out all meaningful opposition to the official version of the Cold War' (Ellen W. Schrecker, *No Ivory Tower: McCarthyism and the Universities* (New York: Oxford University Press, 1986), pp. 339 and 341). See also David Caute, *The Great Fear: The Anti-Communist Purge Under Truman and Eisenhower* (New York: Simon and Schuster, 1978), pp. 403-30, and Lionel S. Lewis, *The Cold War on Campus* (New Brunswick: Transaction Books, 1988).

*A striking illustration of this can be found in Gabriel Almond's contribution to the review of late modernization theory edited by Myron Wiener and Samuel P. Huntington, *Understanding Political Development* (Boston: Little, Brown, 1987), in which he represents the modernization school as 'objective' ('governed by professional criteria of evidence and inference') and its critics as mere propagandists (pp. 444-68 and especially 450 ff.).

to say that 'development theory' was originally just theory about the best way for colonial, and then ex-colonial, states to accelerate national economic growth in this international environment. The goal of development was growth; the agent of development was the state, and the means of development were these macroeconomic policy instruments. These were taken-for-granted presuppositions of 'development theory' as it evolved from the 1950s onwards.

For over ten years (i.e. from 1955 to the late 1960s) 'development theory' so conceived progressed with only modest excitement. Then, partly due to disappointment with the results of policies based on 'development theory' (especially in Latin America and India), and partly to the general reaction of the 1960s against all 'official' values and ideas, the theoretical temperature rose. The a-historical, unselfcritical and politically partisan nature of 'development theory' was put in question by critics on the 'left'; and one way to understand the heady debates that followed throughout most of the 1970s is as a struggle between those who tried to keep 'development theory' within its original parameters, and critics who were trying to extend them and place the issues back into the framework of the historically-oriented and ethical tradition of general development theory founded by Hegel and Marx.

The full implications of doing this were, however, obscured for a long time by the fact that most of the critics also subscribed to a very practical, short-term, state-orientated conception of development (and in many cases were also influenced by Cold War partisanship).*

But the work of finally demonstrating the limitations of mainstream 'development theory' was not left to be accomplished by criticism alone. By the mid-1980s the real world on which 'development theory' had been premised had also disappeared.

---

*E.g. the Maoism of Pierre-Phillippe Rey, in *Les Alliances de classes* (Paris: Maspero, 1973) and the Guevarism of Regis Debray, in *Revolution in the Revolution? Armed Struggle and Political Struggle in Latin America* (New York: Monthly Review Press, 1967).

Above all, national and international controls over capital movements had been removed, drastically curtailing the power of any state wishing to promote national development, while the international 'development community' threw itself into the task of strengthening 'market forces' (i.e. capital) at the expense of states everywhere, but especially in the Third World. As a result most states could no longer be the prime movers of development that 'development theory' had hitherto always presupposed, and none of the alternative candidates (such as 'social movements' or 'communities') proposed by 'development theorists' as the field unravelled was very convincing.

But this is to anticipate. The next section seeks to make more persuasive the general characterization of 'development theory' given above by recalling briefly how the contents of some of the main currents of development theory were determined by who produced them, under what conditions and why.

Development theories: science and discourses[7]

The first formulations of development theory were the work of economists, all strongly influenced by the ideas of Keynes and the wartime and postwar practices of state intervention in the economy, including the perceived success of the Marshall Plan, which was in many ways a model for later ideas about 'aid'. They shared the broadly social-democratic ethos of the period, including its commitment to planning and its conviction that economic problems would yield to the actions of benevolent states endowed with sufficient supplies of capital and armed with good economic analysis. They produced what P.W. Preston aptly called development theory's 'positivist orthodoxy'.[8] They wrote development plans for both newly independent countries and the not yet independent colonies of Africa, based on the idea of raising rural productivity and transferring underutilized labour out of agriculture into industry.

By the end of the 1950s, however, the original optimism that this approach would yield rapid results had begun to evaporate, and the limitations of development economics as a theory of development were beginning to be exposed. The failure of the Indian economy, in particular, to respond rapidly to this approach was attributed in part to the 'softness' of the Indian state, which seemed to lack the capacity to live up to the social-democratic ideal of a rational, firmly benevolent enforcer of the national interest and impose the necessary discipline on everyone from businessmen and landlords to small peasants.[9] But this famous judgement, coming from Gunnar Myrdal and his associates (notably Paul Streeten, and later Dudley Seers), representing the 'left' (and most historically and sociologically sensitive) wing of development economics, signalled the existence of complex problems which lay beyond the conceptual and empirical scope of mainstream – i.e. neo-classical – economics.* Marx had long ago grasped that states were, as he put it, but the 'official resumés' of civil society. In the first phase of development economics this had been forgotten. What was it about these societies that made them unresponsive to the 'positivist orthodoxy'?

'Modernization theory' was an American response to this question. It was constructed by sociologists and political scientists involved in the rapidly expanding research and teaching programmes established by the US government to equip the country with the regional expertise it needed to exercise its new role as a superpower. These experts none the less found themselves largely excluded from policy-making roles in the US Agency for International Development (US AID) or the World Bank, the two most important

---

*Myrdal, who had served for ten years as head of the secretariat of the Economic Commission for Europe, was intensely aware of the limitations of a purely economistic approach to development problems, i.e. one restricted to what can be analysed within the framework of neo-classical economics. He was also keenly aware of the Cold War context, and reading *Asian Drama* makes a painful contrast with what was then being produced in the USA. Myrdal's 'Prologue' ('The Beam in Our Eyes') is a systematic review of the sources of bias in Western development studies and a strong warning against 'opportunist research' - studies that are expected to reach opportune conclusions and to appear in a form that is regarded as advantageous, or at least not disadvantageous, to national interests as these are officially and popularly understood' (p. 12).

aid agencies in the world, both headquartered in Washington; and modernization theory can be understood in part as their explanation of why the plans of development economists who monopolized these organizations so seldom worked. They believed that in the transition from 'traditional' to 'modern' forms of social organization, already completed in the industrialized West, the complex interactions between social change and economic development, mediated by politics, could be traced with some precision, using 'structural-functional analysis' and a typology of social structures derived from Weber by Talcott Parsons. This belief had a fervent quality that survives even in this retrospective summary by one of its most prominent practitioners, David Apter:

> Structural-functional analysis .. .is concerned with the connections between norms, structures, and behaviors, the first in terms of values and interests, the second in terms of roles, role networks, and classes, and the third in terms of motivation and perception. An equilibrium model, its political focus is on the stability of complementary and mutually reinforcing relations between each of the dimensions. The three together constitute a system. Change in any one will effect alterations in the others... Within these abstract formulations it is possible to organise highly complex masses of data around a host of subsidiary variables ... There is a clarity in this framework and, if it is used with a certain austerity, a theoretical power lacking in some of the work of those who attacked it.*

Practically, the modernization theorists envisaged modern values being diffused through education and technology transfer to the 'elites' of the periphery. Some attention was paid to this idea in aid policies, especially through technical assistance and scholarship programmes, but on the whole its influence on policy was minor. The modernization school had a bigger impact on academic research,

---

*David E. Apter, writing with Carl G. Rosberg, in 'Changing African Perspectives', in Apter and Rosberg (eds.), *Political Development and the New Reality in Sub-Saharan Africa* (Charlottesville: University Press of Virginia, 1994), pp. 22-23. The claim to superior clarity and theoretical power that is made here for modernization theory is, to say the least, debatable. The authors do acknowledge, however, that the modernization 'paradigm' had 'some fundamental flaws', including the assumption that each country would progress unproblematically towards modernity, and that the role of external forces would be benign.

although this owed more to the important topics they opened up by their well-funded fieldwork – topics such as political parties, social movements and the dynamics of social change, whose study had not been encouraged by the former colonial authorities – than to their methodology. And, although the influence of Max Weber on their work was transmitted in the schematized form of Talcott Parsons's 'pattern variables', it had some valuable consequences; for example, some modernization research took seriously the persistence of pre-capitalist social relations and cultural practices, issues that were largely neglected by the modernization school's critics in the 1970s.*

But modernization theory suffered from defects closely connected with its leading exponents' place in the scheme of things. As Irene Gendzier has pointed out, they were mostly closely connected to the American state and accepted its purposes, including its intense preoccupation with combating communism.[10] Some modernization theorists were serious cold warriors – Gabriel Almond, Edward Shils, Lucien Pye and Samuel Huntington, for example; others merely accepted the Cold War and were content to see themselves as the 'liberal' wing of American development studies, believing that modernization would in any case bring democracy as well as economic growth. Very few at that time publicly questioned the identification of modernization studies with the aims of US foreign policy. In the 1950s and early 1960s the Central Intelligence Agency (CIA) regularly 'debriefed' US scholars returning from Third World fieldwork and the State Department frequently sought their advice. This situation also led to a 'symptomatic silence' about the social character of development, a silence cloaked, perhaps, by the doctrine of 'value-freedom'. It was implicit that the development under discussion was not socialist, but its capitalist character was not acknowledged either; it was just 'development', and was certainly

---

*In this respect a writer whose work deserved more respect than it got from the left in these years was Fred Riggs, especially his initial study, *Administration in Developing Countries: The Theory of Prismatic Society* (Boston: Mifflin, 1964).

not seen as prone to generate class formation and conflict, or as inherently uneven or crisis-ridden.

The shortcomings of modernization theory were first attacked where they were most plainly apparent – in Latin America, which had enjoyed formal independence for more than a century, but had still to enjoy the fruits that according to modernization theory ought long since to have flowed from it. Or, rather, they were attacked from within Latin America by the German-American Andre Gunder Frank, arriving in Chile from the USA in 1962, using the concepts of dependency and underdevelopment. Dependency theory was not invented by Frank, although he played a leading part in its formulation in Latin America in the 1960s; it was implicit in a long tradition of Latin American historiography, which Frank cited extensively, and also in the structuralist analysis developed at the Economic Commission for Latin America under Raul Prebisch in the 1950s. But Frank was uniquely qualified and motivated to deploy the concepts of dependency against modernization theory, the politics of which he had left the USA to escape.[11]

Even before the naive optimism of much early modernization theory had been exposed by the end of the post-war boom and the deepening US involvement in Vietnam and other anti-communist ventures, Frank's polemical assaults, coinciding with the student revolt of the 1960s, had effectively demolished its pretensions to scientificity.*

The early 1970s thus became – briefly – an era of dependency theory. Or, to be more accurate, in intellectual circles, especially among students in Europe and in Third World countries, dependency theory held the initiative; and eventually even the international 'development community' felt obliged to accommodate some of its

---

*Especially 'Sociology of Development and Underdevelopment of Sociology', first published in 1967, and the other articles collected in *Latin America: Underdevelopment or Revolution?* (New York: Monthly Review Press, 1969), reprinted six times. It is interesting how little the US modernization school establishment felt it necessary to respond to their critics, in spite of the effectiveness of the critique in sidelining modernization thinking outside the USA.

perspectives: for instance, the International Labour Office's 1972 call for 'redistribution with growth', and the World Bank's adoption in 1973 of the principle of meeting 'basic needs' were both influenced by the (unacknowledged) impact of dependency thinking.*

Dependency theory inverted many of the assumptions of modernization theory. It saw metropolitan policy as maleficent, not beneficent; inflows of foreign investment were seen as giving rise to much greater interest and profit outflows; 'modernizing elites' were really 'compradores', or 'lumpenbourgeoisies', serving their own and foreign interests, not those of the people; world trade perpetuated structures of underdevelopment, rather than acting as a solvent of them. Capitalist development ('development' now had a label, at least for 'left' dependency theorists) offered nothing to the periphery; the solution lay in reducing links to the metropoles and bringing about 'autocentric' national economic growth.

There were wide differences within dependency theory, of course. 'Bourgeois' dependency theorists in Latin America, such as Osvaldo Sunkel or Celso Furtado, could perhaps be considered (however unfairly, in terms of their actual party-political sympathies) 'organic intellectuals' of their own national capitalist class, chafing at its subordination to the interests of foreign companies and the influence of the US state in domestic politics. Radical or 'left'

---

*The prime movers in the former initiative were Hans (the late Sir Hans) Singer and Richard Jolly, who led the team responsible for *Employment, Incomes and Equality: A Strategy for Increasing Productive Employment in Kenya* (Geneva: ILO, 1972). Singer and Jolly were both at the Institute of Development Studies (IDS) at the University of Sussex, which bridged (sometimes uneasily) the worlds of academia and practical policy-making in the Third World; at various times the IDS was home to a number of dependency theorists including Manfred Bienefeld, Raphael Kaplinsky, Henry Bernstein and myself. The 'basic needs' initiative came from within the staff of the World Bank, and especially Hollis Chenery; it was officially propounded in 1973 in a speech to the Board of Governors of the Bank meeting in Nairobi by the then president of the Bank, Robert McNamara. Of course it would be absurd to attribute too much influence to dependency theory as such. It was rather that the growing realization that the hopes of rapid and widespread development were going to be disappointed, and sympathy for the masses in the ex-colonies and fear of their reactions, had been better anticipated by the discourse of dependency, which by this time had become influential everywhere in the Third World.

dependency theorists such as T. Dos Santos and Rui Mauro Marini, on the other hand, aligned themselves openly with the Latin American labour movements, or with radical parties such as the MIR in Chile, and paid a high price by losing their jobs, being forced into exile or even being murdered during the era of the military dictatorships.* But both tendencies had one thing in common, which separated them from all the other schools of development theory so far discussed: their intellectual debt to Marx and Hegel. Their critique of official development thinking rested fundamentally on a pulling away from the short-term, ahistorical and uncritical perspectives of Western-produced, state-orientated development discourse, towards the perspective of a 'universal history'.

But these thinkers themselves also believed that the countries of the 'periphery' could somehow, through better theory and different political leadership, jump over the barriers placed in their way by history, and this gave rise to some key ambiguities in their thought: above all, their tendency to assume the availability of some unspecified alternative development path, more equitable and less painful, which was not – in the absence of stronger and more mobilized social forces at the periphery, and more sympathetic support from abroad – really available.[12] This problem persisted, even when Frank's early version of dependency theory, according to which development was always systematically blocked at the periphery, had been generally abandoned in favour of the idea that,

---

*Some dependency theorists in Latin America who were persecuted under the military dictatorships were supported by foundations and universities in the USA, producing a particular kind of accommodation between Latin American neo-Marxism and American liberalism. The Brazilian dependentista Fernando Henrique Cardoso, who would later, as President of Brazil, come to an accommodation with global capital, was a leading example of this; he was very early on considered the 'right' sort of Marxist by leading US academics concerned with the challenge of Marxism. His book with Enzo Faletto, *Dependency and Development in Latin America* (Berkeley: University of California Press, 1979), was rightly seen as a model of the creative use of a neo-Marxist conceptual framework for analysing the diverse 'concrete situations of dependency', which did not commit the authors to a particular political line and managed to combine inspiring flourishes with a generally dispassionate tone.

while it was always necessarily difficult, dependent on external forces and 'distorted' (Cardoso's famous 'associated dependent development'), development might none the less sometimes be possible.[13]

In sub-Saharan Africa, dependency theory was broadly accepted by many foreign Africanists and many, perhaps most, African social scientists, not to mention educated people in general, and especially the youth; but there was a further problem, that outside the Republic of South Africa the level of development in few countries had yet produced either a local 'national' capitalist class or a local labour movement (or indeed any other modern social movement) that had the capacity to lead national development along any alternative development path, even if such a path could be plausibly specified.* As a moral critique of existing policy in Africa, dependency theory played a significant role. But except in Nyerere's Tanzania dependency thinking was not adopted as an explicit basis for policy, and the problems of Tanzanian socialism had many sources besides the inherent shortcomings of dependency theory.

In any case, it was not shortcomings revealed in practice that led to the most significant critiques of dependency theory.** Critics from the right generally failed to make the effort needed to understand the Marxian problematique from which many of dependency theory's key ideas were drawn, so as to be able to make

---

*This judgement may seem to ignore the potential of Africa's peasantries, especially those who were forced into prolonged armed liberation struggles; and it may well be that history will judge the defeats inflicted on these peasantries' aspirations by global forces in the 1980s as one of the most crucial contributions to the continent's end-of-the-century morass. For the time being, however, the original potential of Africa's peasant-based socialist projects is very hard to assess with any confidence.

**The statist development strategies that were adopted by socialist governments in Guinée, Ghana, Mozambique and elsewhere were mostly informed as much by neo-Stalinist ideas about development, contributed by East European aid personnel, as by dependency theory, although in each case the mix was complex and the outcomes less predictable than they are often made to seem in retrospect. The Tanzanian experience did eventually become a focus for critics of dependency theory but only long after the debate had been initiated on more general grounds.

effective attacks on it (this was particularly evident in the attempts to use cross-national statistical data to prove, for example, that periphery country growth rates were not inversely related to trade links with the countries of the 'core').[14] The most damaging criticism came rather from the 'classical Marxist' left.*

These critics were, ironically enough, probably the nearest thing we now have to 'traditional intellectuals', in Gramsci's sense of the term (i.e. a category of intellectuals not linked to either of the main contending classes). Their mostly marginal position, even in European academic life (not to mention the USA, where even in the mid-1970s few campuses would give them a home), tended to detach them from metropolitan social forces and interests concerned with the Third World; while the fact that they were typically not engaged as consultants meant that many of them, after an initial period of teaching at some Third World university, tended to become separated from social forces and interests in Third World countries as well. Writers like Geoffrey Kay, Giovanni Arrighi, Arghiri Emmanuel, Michael Cowen and Bill Warren often seemed to display the attachment of the political exile (in their case, exile from the academic and policy-making mainstream) to theory as such. While this had its disadvantages, it did enable them to make a trenchant critique of the eclecticism, populism and practical ambiguity of dependency theory: now for the first time 'development theory' of the post-war variety was squarely confronted from the perspective of the historical tradition of development theory derived from Hegel and Marx.

To take a well-known early example, in 1975 Geoffrey Kay showed that dependentistas who accused the metropoles of 'exploiting' the periphery rarely had a very clear idea of what they meant by this. Marx, in contrast, had formulated a clear concept according to which capitalist exploitation referred to the

*I use the term 'classical' here, rather than 'orthodox', which has pejorative overtones, to designate those Marxists who saw themselves as applying, and perhaps extending, but not radically revising or modifying Marxist theory.

appropriation by the owners of capital of the surplus value produced by workers; and the more surplus value they produced, the greater the rate of exploitation. The most exploited workers, on this analysis, are those that produce most surplus value, and they are the ones who work with most capital, such as the highly paid workers of the US automobile industry. Therefore the real problem of the Third World, Kay maintained, was not that it was super-exploited, but that it was not exploited enough.[15]

Like many of the theses advanced by the classical Marxists in their contributions to development theory, however, this was a 'Menshevik' kind of argument, in the sense that it seemed to imply that capitalist development of the periphery was a necessary prelude to socialism: not a political stance that appealed to many people on the left, inside or outside the Third World, who in any case did not believe it would happen. This was a central difficulty in the classical Marxist position and it was compounded, rather than resolved, by the position eventually adopted by Bill Warren, who argued in his book *Imperialism: Pioneer of Capitalism*, published posthumously in 1980, that capitalism was in fact developing rapidly throughout the Third World, and accomplishing its 'civilizing' mission there into the bargain.* This hardly corresponded to what many people in the Third World (and especially in Africa) seemed to be experiencing, and certainly not to the feelings most people had about capitalist development, even in places (such as, for example, India or Mexico) where it might seem to be occurring. Perhaps Warren, had he lived to revise his book for publication, would have avoided giving the impression that capitalist development could be expected to develop

---

*Warren seems to have seen his position as Leninist, i.e. Bolshevik, rather than Menshevik, to judge from his strong endorsement of Lenin's position in the debate with the populists and the Mensheviks in Russia (Bill Warren, *Imperialism: Pioneer of Capitalism* (London: Verso, 1980)), pp. 30-39. But his unfinished text gave the impression that he held the wholly implausible view that Russia's development trajectory down to 1917 was bound to be repeated throughout the Third World in the 1980s and 1990s.

the entire world, and soon. As it was, his text bent the stick much too far in the opposite direction from the early dependency line.

Marxist development theorists were also frequently attacked for being 'Eurocentric', especially for applying to backward societies categories like that of 'the working class', which did not apply there, and neglecting phenomena like ethnicity, which did. On the whole, this was a canard. The real issue was how far capitalist development was forming classes, and how far this cut across ethnic and other pre-capitalist solidarities. In practice, the empirical studies conducted by Marxist researchers were no more Eurocentric than those of their critics.

No, the real problem of the Marxists' contribution to development theory was not so much that their analysis was wrong; in many ways they appear in retrospect to have maintained a rather objective stance, relative to the various other schools, helped by the broad historical perspective and understanding of capitalist dynamics that they drew from Marx. Their crucial problem was rather that there were too few people in the Third World, and virtually none in tropical Africa, for whom the political and moral standpoint of their analysis – i.e. that people should struggle against capitalist development, while not expecting to transcend it until it had first been accomplished – made sense. Their perspective was, to say the least, very long-term, and offered no plausible line of immediate political action to improve matters.* The fact that

---

*Gavin Kitching made a characteristically honest attempt to face this issue when he said: 'I believe that a socialist alternative to capitalism in Africa can be constructed by a sophisticated socialist movement created among the working classes of Africa as they slowly expand through time... I believe, however, that the formation of a sophisticated socialist working class in Africa will take a long time and that a prolonged period of struggle against a developing capitalism there is one of the important prerequisites of its creation. To that extent I am "happy" to see continued capitalist development in Black Africa (though this may or may not occur)' ('Politics. Method and Evidence in the "Kenya Debate"', in Henry Bernstein and Bonnie K. Campbell (eds.), *Contradictions of Accumulation in Africa* (Beverly Hills: Sage, 1985), pp. 147-48. African readers of this might well wonder how socialism would come about if continued capitalist development, against which they should be struggling, did not in fact occur to the point where a 'sophisticated working class' existed.

'mainstream' development theory had consistently failed to produce results did not make the Marxist view any better in this respect.*

A more plausible political position was, of course, that of the neo-liberals, who did not believe that capitalism would give way to socialism and were only interested in accelerating its advance in the Third World. They believed that what was blocking or retarding this was none of the things highlighted by all the theories so far discussed, but rather the whole idea of bringing about development through state intervention in the economy in the first place. This was the standpoint of P.T. (later Lord) Bauer, Deepak Lal, Bela Balassa, Ian Little and others, who represented in development theory the neo-liberal revolution that was taking place in the metropoles at the end of the 1970s, and who offered an intellectual justification for a new wave of market-oriented intervention by the World Bank and the IMF. The older representatives of this current belonged to a small group of economists who opposed the post-war social-democratic consensus and who were, as a result, almost as exiled from the mainstream as the Marxists (although sustained over the years, as Radhika Desai showed, by membership in a sect-like network organized by the Mont Pelerin Society, the American Enterprise Institute and the Institute of Economic Affairs).[16] They argued that development was blocked by inflated public sectors, distorting economic controls and overemphasis on capital formation. Governments were part of the problem, not part of the solution; they were inefficient and often corrupt and hence parasitic,

---

*For an engaging discussion of the spurious and self-interested demand often made by some members of the 'development community', that critical theorists of development should come up with an answer to the question of 'what is to be done?', see James Ferguson, *The Anti-Politics Machine: 'Development', Depoliticization, and Bureaucratic Power in Lesotho* (Cambridge: Cambridge University Press, 1990), pp. 279–88. Members of the 'development industry', he remarks, 'seek only the kind of advice they can take. One "developer" asked my advice on what his country could do "to help these people". When I suggested that his government might contemplate sanctions against apartheid, he replied, with predictable irritation, "No, no! I mean development!" The only "advice" that is in question here is advice about how to "do development" better' (p. 284).

not stimulators of growth. The solution was to privatize the public sector, reduce the scale and scope of government spending and give up all policies, from exchange rate controls to subsidies and redistributive taxation, that altered any prices that would otherwise be set by the impersonal forces of the market.

As John Toye pointed out, the neo-liberals' success in relation to the Third World owed a good deal to the fact that they were ready to say openly what others in the 'development community' knew perfectly well but had (unlike the dependency theorists) been unwilling to say, out of an anxiety not to jeopardize relations between Third World governments and the development agencies for which they worked: namely, that these governments were never exclusively concerned to promote the development goals they were ostensibly committed to, and quite often were not committed to them at all.[17]

There was also a strong core of justification for their criticisms of the public sector and of government practices in most Third World countries. But, as Toye also showed, this common-sense criticism did not add up to a theoretical justification for the neo-liberals' claims about the benefits that would flow from an unrestricted market. These claims were very poorly supported with evidence, and were often prima facie implausible; they sprang rather from a deep ideological hostility to government in general, and especially to the legitimacy which the doctrine of state intervention gave to socialists or even social-democrats in office.

In any case it was not the shortcomings of the principal existing schools of development theory, serious as they were, that made possible the ascendancy of neo-liberalism (whose shortcomings were quickly revealed as no less serious). What made possible the triumph of neo-liberalism in mainstream development thinking was material, not ideal: the radical transformation in both the structure and the management of the world economy that had begun in the 1960s, and which finally seemed to offer the possibility of creating for the first time in history a truly unified global capitalist economy

– and one regulated, if at all, only by institutions reflecting the interests of transnational capital. Neo-liberalism articulated the goals and beliefs of the dominant forces that stood to benefit from this process, and pushed it forward. Social-democratic parties and labour movements tried to resist it, but the 'new right' succeeded in neutralizing this resistance and initiating its own market-oriented project in one industrial country after another. The 'development community', which was either part of the state apparatuses of these countries or depended critically on them for funding, was bound to come into line.

But although the 'development community' was loath to acknowledge it, the new global economic regime thoroughly undermined the foundations of development theory as it had hitherto been conceived.

The real world of development

The world in which Keynesian policy-making – and its offshoots, development economics and development theory – made sense had changed fundamentally. It is true that in some respects the world economy at the end of the 1980s was less integrated than it had been at the beginning of the century, and there were significant tendencies towards protectionism, offsetting those towards a single worldwide market. But relative to the situation that existed between 1945 and the late 1960s, the changes were fundamental.

World trade as a share of world output had returned to the general level of 1913 (i.e. up from 7% of total gross domestic product (GDP) in 1945 to 15% in 1988); foreign direct investment had risen to account for significant shares of total investment (5-10% of capital stock) in most major economies; and about a third of all trade between countries had come to consist of the movement of goods between different national branches of one or another multinational company. The mutual dependence of national economies implied by these facts was significant (obviously, it is not necessary for half of a country's capital assets to be foreign owned for decisions taken in foreign countries to have a major impact on its fortunes); but even more striking was the internationalization of capital flows. Instead of merely financing world trade, by the end of the 1980s banks and non-bank financial institutions were dealing in currency exchanges, currency and commodity futures and so-called 'derivatives' of all sorts on a scale that not only dwarfed the conventional transactions needed for trade and investment, but made it impossible for the governments of even large economies to influence the value of their currency by intervening in the currency markets.*

But in the meantime control of capital movements had in any case also been abandoned as a deliberate policy decision, promoted, above all, by the USA. As competition with other industrial countries intensified, the USA borrowed abroad and became the world's largest debtor nation. As such it was obliged to give up its commitment to meet its dollar obligations in gold, which it did in 1971; and eventually, in 1973, the Bretton Woods system of fixed exchange rates was abandoned altogether. This opened up new opportunities for international currency speculation and led to a new period of extreme instability in currency values and commodity prices, including the oil price increases of the 1970s and 1980s; these in turn led to vast new dollar balances being accumulated by the oil-exporting countries, and correspondingly vast expansions of borrowing, which drove up the total of international debt to previously unheard-of levels.

The abandonment of the post-war international trading regime was followed in 1979-80 by the abandonment of Keynesian economic policy in the OECD countries, led by the UK and the

---

*A classic example was provided by the collapse of the exchange rate mechanism (ERM) of the then European Community in September 1992, when the British government tried to maintain the pound sterling in the ERM by the traditional expedient of using the country's reserves of foreign currencies to buy pounds and so create a demand for them, to offset the selling by speculators counting on forcing a devaluation. The government spent several billion pounds in less than two days in this effort: the volume of currencies traded on the world's currency exchanges on an average day at that time was three trillion dollars.

USA. Deregulation in the USA and deregulation and privatization in the UK were accompanied by high interest rates. The governments of the other European industrial countries followed suit, either willingly or (in the case of France) because keeping interest rates significantly below those of other countries led to capital outflows that could no longer be prevented – 'Keynesianism in one country' was no longer practicable. Capital exports were formally deregulated in the UK in 1979 and de facto everywhere else by the mid-1980s. Then, at the end of 1993, the conclusion of the 'Uruguay Round' of the GATT negotiations inaugurated a further extension of global free trade, including the formerly sacrosanct agricultural sector, while further reductions in the regulatory powers of most industrial country governments were imposed by the European Union's Single Market and Maastricht Treaties and the North American Free Trade Agreement.

These changes did not succeed in restoring growth rates to the levels achieved after the Second World War. From the late 1960s the average rate of growth of the OECD countries fell from the post-war level of 3-4% to around 2%. The developing countries inevitably followed suit, except that there was now a growing polarization among them. Besides the four East Asian 'newly industrialized countries' (which accounted for half of the entire Third World's exports of manufactures), in the 1980s China and, to a lesser extent, India began to grow faster, while the other developing countries slowed down – in the recession that began in the late 1970s their average growth rate declined and in 1983 even became negative.* Lower growth rates in the OECD countries and intensified competition also adversely affected the Third World countries' terms

---

*According to the Bank's *World Development Report* for 1994, the low income countries as a whole, excluding China and India, experienced an average annual per capita growth rate of 1.2% between 1980 and 1992, while the middle-income countries had an average annual decline of 0.1 %. By regions, per capita incomes in sub-Saharan Africa declined by 0.8% a year on average in the same period, in the Middle East and North Africa they declined by 2.3%, and in Latin America and the Caribbean by 0.2%.

of trade and interest rates: for the 1980s, 'in Sub-Saharan Africa and Latin America the combined effects [of declining terms of trade and interest rate increases] were estimated to average more than 10 percent of GDP'.[18]

Most Third World countries, then, found themselves more vulnerable than at any time since they were first colonized. Their economies were least well placed to prosper in the new 'global' market place. Primary commodity exports, other than oil, became steadily less significant as manufacturing became less commodity-intensive, and the overall share of the Third World in world trade fell dramatically. Faced with stagnating economies, and with per capita incomes declining from levels at which many people could barely survive already, they responded by increased borrowing abroad until servicing the debt led to balance of payments difficulties so acute that they were forced to turn to the IMF. As a condition of further support the IMF and the World Bank then forced them to cut back government intervention in their economies, leaving them instead to be revived by the freer play of 'market forces'. This did not, of course, produce the anticipated results. Per capita incomes fell still further in all the affected countries (in sub-Saharan Africa, by over a quarter), while the debt-service burden (the proportion of export earnings spent on capital repayments and interest) of the 'low-income countries' (excluding China and India) rose from 11.8% in 1980 to 24.5% in 1992.[19] The overall effects are well summed up by Glyn and Sutcliffe:

> The share of Africa, Asia and Latin America in world trade is now substantially lower than before 1913. This reflects a major decline in the relative importance of tropical raw materials in world trade... This long-term structural reason for the decline... has been joined in the period since 1973 by a major short-term crisis in many poorer countries... Latin America's share of world exports fell from 12.4 percent in 1950 to 5.5 percent in 1980 and only 3.9 percent in 1990; Asia's was 13.1 percent in 1950, rose to 17.8 percent in 1980 and fell back again to 14 percent in 1990. And Africa's share all but disappeared: in 1950 it was 5.2 percent, in 1980 4.7 percent and in 1990 only 1.9 percent. In 1955 exports from Africa were three times

those of Japan; by 1986 the exports of Japan were four times the exports of Africa. The picture for international investment is rather similar. Between 1950 and 1980 the share of all foreign investment going to the Third World held roughly constant at about 25 percent. But after 1984 the share fell sharply to well under 20 percent... [and] is very unequally distributed. It goes in significant quantities to only a few resource-rich countries and the newly industrialising countries (including China) while the so-called 'least developed countries' are increasingly excluded. In the second half of the 1980s this group received only 0.1 percent of all foreign investment. ...Once again Africa and most of Latin America and some Asian countries are failing to participate in the growing globalisation of the rest of the world... they are increasingly marginalised within the system of which they form a part.[20]

The story of the world economy under liberalization could, of course, be given a rosy gloss, as in the following excerpt from a *Washington Post* editorial:

The rise of wealth in the late 20th century has been more sustained and more widespread than ever before in history ... Economic growth is measured in dollars, but it translates into other and much more important things – better health and longer lives, less harsh physical labor, greater economic security. There are drawbacks, like development's threats to the environment and the dismaying tendency of governments to spend too much of their new wealth on weapons. But it is hardly Pollyannaish to say that the balance remains strongly in favor of the essential human values.[21]

Admittedly, to take this line involves overlooking the implications of many of the data reviewed in the last few paragraphs, not to mention the serious risk of conflicts within or between countries of the former 'First' or 'Second' Worlds as the impact of global competition drives whole districts, regions or even countries into permanent poverty, while others prosper. But for present purposes it does not really matter: even on the most optimistic view this picture leaves little or no room for 'development theory' as it used to be conceived.

The era of national economies and national economic strategies is past – for the time being, at least. With capital free to move where it wishes, no state (and least of all a small poor one) can pursue any economic policy that the owners of capital seriously dislike. Economic planning, welfare systems and fiscal and monetary policies all became subject to control, in effect, by the capital markets, signalled, in the case of Third World countries, by the conditions attached to IMF/World Bank lending – precisely the situation the Bretton Woods system was designed to prevent. And in the Third World the whole thrust of IMF/World Bank policy, imposed through the conditions attached to almost two hundred structural-adjustment lending programmes and reinforced by bilateral lending consortia, was to reduce still further the power of national governments to act as prime movers of development. Instead of reforming inefficient agencies, structural adjustment policies tended to emasculate or eliminate them. Parastatals have been privatized, without thereby becoming more effective. It is hardly too much to say that by the end of the 1980s the only development policy that was officially approved was not to have one – to leave it to the market to allocate resources, not the state. In the World Bank's own ingenuous language, 'New ideas stress prices as signals; trade and competition as links to technical progress; and effective government as a scarce resource, to be employed sparingly and only where most needed.'*

Individual national governments – especially in the smaller underdeveloped countries, with which development theory used to be above all concerned – thus no longer have the tools at their disposal to manage their domestic economies so as to accelerate growth, foster industrialization and 'catch up', as development theory

---

*This revealing formulation comes from the conclusions of the World Bank's review of 'the evolution of approaches to development' in its 1991 *World Development Report*, under the heading 'The Way Forward'. As the real consequences of structural adjustment became inescapably obvious towards the end of the 1980s, especially in Africa, official policy veered back towards an emphasis on the importance of the state, but without reconciling this with the continued official emphasis on the superiority of markets over state action - in a word, official policy became contradictory, as any thoughtful reader of the 1991 *World Development Report* can see.

originally envisaged, and theories premissed on their existence become irrelevant; for most of them Gunder Frank's comment was painfully accurate: 'Now neo-liberalism, post-Keynesianism, and neo-structuralism have... become totally irrelevant and bankrupt for development policy. In the real world, the order of the day has become only economic or debt crisis management.'[22]

Most observers accept that significant parts of the former Third World, including most of sub-Saharan Africa, are more likely to regress than to advance in the new global economy; it is in the nature of an unregulated competitive system that this will happen. Not every country has the capacity to compete in the market; a few will succeed, while others will decline and some will collapse into civil war or anarchy, as Uganda, Somalia, Angola, Mozambique, Liberia and Rwanda already have, in Africa, at different times.

A measure of just how profoundly the world has changed may be had by comparing this reality with the following optimistic words written by Sir Arthur Lewis, one of the founding figures of development economics, as late as 1983:

> All LDCs [less developed countries] are menaced since 1973 by the international recession, by rising protectionism in the industrial countries, by the high price of oil, and by the enormous debt this has created. These disasters are beyond their control and call for special measures by the whole international community. But the viability of LDCs in normal times, like the 1950s and the 1960s, is now beyond doubt.[23]

We can now see that the 1950s and 1960s were not 'normal' times but, on the contrary, a special interlude in the history of the worldwide expansion of capitalism in which 'development theory' could be born, but outside which it could not survive.

This is not to say that theorizing development is no longer possible or necessary; we need theoretical maps of our increasingly integrated world. But we can no longer assume, as all the principal varieties of 'development theory' did, who the agents of collective action for change will be, or that means exist for them to accomplish anything. Perhaps states, acting singly or in groups, will rediscover the means, but this too must be part of the task of theory to establish. In the meantime, we must recognize that an era is closed, that development theory must return to its classical roots and that the relation between theory and practice that has been assumed hitherto (i.e. theory in the service of this or that existing or imagined coalition of political forces in control of a state) has been put radically in question.

'Development theory' faced with the end of its raison d'être
The authors of the World Bank's annual World Development Reports dealt with the problem by ploughing ahead with an increasingly incoherent discourse of opposites: the state is needed, after all, but not too much, and only when the market doesn't work well; democracy is important but not if it leads to inappropriate demands for redistribution;* and so on. Academic development theorists could hardly follow suit, but what could they do instead?

It was not until towards the end of the 1980s that the full significance of the changed environment began to be registered in the theoretical literature, although the drastic reduction in the official goals of development propounded by the World Bank and other agencies over the years had signalled it clearly enough. By the early 1970s the vision of 'catching up' (culminating, in Rostow's 1960 version, in a 'high mass-consumption' society, which implicitly included 'equity' and democracy) had already given way to more modest ambitions: 'redistribution with growth' – i.e. some reduction in inequality, but financed out of growth so that the better off in the developing countries might be less unwilling to agree to it – in a word, fewer illusions about democracy. And by the end of the 1970s redistribution had given way to just trying to meet the 'basic needs'

---

*For a scathing analysis of the 'development community's' attitude to democracy see Gerald G. Schmitz, 'Democratization and Demystification: Deconstructing "Governance" as Development Paradigm', in Moore and Schmitz, (eds.) *Debating Development Discourse*, op. cit., pp. 30-51. The World Bank's annual Development Reports, in particular, came more and more to resemble flip charts for neo-liberal propaganda, a sad decline for what was once, for all its faults, a formidable intellectual machine.

of the poor, who, it seemed, would always be with us after all; the goal of equity had disappeared. Then came structural adjustment; to get growth, underdeveloped societies were to adjust themselves to the procrustean bed allocated to them by the market, and for this purpose even basic needs must be sacrificed.

By then, however, everyone was aware that things had radically changed and that 'development theory' was in deep trouble. Apart from neo-liberalism itself, five main lines of theoretical response can be identified. One was to see the problem as essentially one of theory itself: there is a theoretical 'impasse', which must be overcome by better concepts and research. A second response might be called 'eclecticism as usual in the development community'. A third consisted of further evolutions of dependency theory. A fourth response was to return to the unfinished agenda of Myrdal and the 'neo-institutionalists' of the 1960s – i.e., how to 'add' social and political dimensions on to the analyses of development economics – but this time by analysing these dimensions in terms of rational choice theory. A fifth response, and the last to be considered here, was to renounce any commitment to development, seeking (often in the name of post-structuralism) merely to 'understand' what goes on.

Let us look briefly at these, taking one or two representative thinkers in each case.

'Development studies' as a substitute for development theory ?

In 1991 a group of left-inclined development theorists collaborated to produce an excellent volume, edited by Frans Schuurman, called *Beyond the Impasse: New Directions in Development Theory*.[24] The idea of an 'impasse' in critical development theory had been canvassed in various articles of the mid-1980s, including one by David Booth;[25] by 1991, however, Booth, in a leading contribution to the Schuurman volume, saw signs that the impasse was being overcome. In his view (strongly endorsed by Schuurman) empirical research had emancipated itself from the excessive generality, necessitarianism, teleology, class reductionism, dogmatism and other shortcomings of Marxist-influenced development theory, and in doing so had begun to show a potential for fresh theoretical initiatives. New theory would be sensitive to the great diversity of situations in the Third World, would refuse to reduce complex and locally specific gender and other relations to relations of class, and would allow for the possibility of 'room for manoeuvre' at the 'micro' and 'meso' levels of action, as well as the 'macro' level which had been the focus of previous development theory – without, however, abandoning the inherited agenda of political economy. It might also, Booth hoped, succeed in combining the study of the cultural meanings subjectively attributed to things by people with the study of those same things from an external or objective standpoint, in a way not achieved before: and it would try to be relevant to the concerns of those engaged in practical development work.

Booth's starting-point – the enormous expansion of field research under the aegis of 'development studies' – was, of course, valid; and if we add to this the no less impressive accumulation of social research not necessarily conceived of as 'development studies' – including social and economic history and gender studies in Third World countries – both the volume and the quality have clearly outstripped what went before, frequently revealing the somewhat shaky empirical foundations of much previous 'grand theory' as well. And Booth's characterization of this work as mostly free from some of the vices of earlier development thinking – reductionism, excessive generality and the rest – and as being much more varied in its interests, was also accurate. Women's roles, local-level activity, ethnicity, religion and culture, for example, which all tended to be secondary in the earlier literature, are often fore-grounded in more recent work, which also tends to show more concern for detail, sets higher standards of proof and is in many ways intellectually refreshing.

But Booth's idea that new development theory will emerge autogenetically from the accumulating volume and density of all this work, through some spontaneous fusion with the concerns of previous political economy, is a different matter. On the one hand, these 'mini-narratives' (if one may so call them, in contrast to the old 'big meta-narratives' which it is now fashionable to disclaim) have implicit higher-level theoretical presuppositions that need to be made explicit (microfoundations imply macrostructures, as much as the other way round), and it would be surprising if these were found to constitute, so to speak spontaneously, a new and better theory of development. And, even more crucially, the construction of a new theory of development is necessarily a political task, involving political choices about whom (what social forces) the theory is for, to accomplish what ends and in what contexts. Conflicting political commitments were, after all, what ultimately inspired the powerful theoretical debates within 'development theory' in the 1970s, and any worthwhile renewal of development theory now depends on a renewed clarification of political presuppositions and purposes as well.

To put it another way, what is striking about the way Booth and his colleagues conceived of the 'impasse' and its transcendence is that it was so idealist: i.e. the origins and the solution of the problem seemed to lie in theory itself. With the exception of a page in Schuurman's 'Introduction', little reference was made in the book to the changes in the real world that had undercut the original development project. There was unease about what 'development' now meant, and the authors presumably agreed with Schuurman's disclaimer that the goal cannot be 'one grand and glorious metatheory'. But they did not confront the thought that, so long as collective socio-economic interests are supposed to be the products of the action of market forces, rather than goals of strategic state action, the domain of 'development theory' is radically changed, if not abolished; that what is left is simply a world economy whose effects are overwhelmingly determined by very powerful states and market actors, with at most minor modifications or delays brought about by the actions of lesser states, social movements, communities or whatever, which do not have significant military or market power. Certainly, this thought may be mistaken, or at least exaggerated; but in that case a new theory of development must at least begin by showing why.

To repeat what was said earlier, this is not to say that there is no further use for theory. But theory needs both a subject and an object, and the prerequisite of any new development theory that aims to be practical must surely be the analysis of the now deregulated global market and the social forces that dominate it, and then a definition of alternative social forces whose developmental needs cannot be met within this system, and which can be expected to struggle against it. Simply abjuring the alleged shortcomings of the theories that were constructed in the period of the collectively-regulated world economy of legally sovereign states, and accumulating ever more detailed and subtle empirical analyses of local and particular experiences, will not of itself answer this need; for that world economy is, as Hegel put it, a form of life that has become old, and which theory cannot rejuvenate but only understand.

Eclecticism as usual in the development community?

The term 'development community' refers here to the network of people professionally concerned with development – the staff of 'donor' and recipient country development ministries, of multilateral 'aid' agencies, financial institutions and non-government organizations, and academic and non-academic consultants. It implies no disrespect to say that this community also constitutes an interest which has to adapt as best it can to constantly changing circumstances, rather like civil servants at the national level. There is a broad consensus about aims and possibilities, founded on development economics but honed by experience and the perspectives of other disciplines into a somewhat eclectic mixture capable of absorbing sometimes quite drastic changes in fashion or politics (witness, for example, the World Bank's successive accommodations, first to a mild touch of dependency, and then, within a decade, to neo-liberalism); and then, when the need passes, reverting back to a more centrist stance. How has the development community responded to the new situation?

As an example we may take John Toye's widely-acclaimed study, *Dilemmas of Development*.[26] Toye's book is well known as a trenchant critique of the neo-liberal dogma which gained ascendancy in the World Bank and IMF in the 1980s, but it is also quite a revealing statement of his own position. For, besides criticizing the neo-liberals, Toye also criticizes the old political economy ('left wing', in his terminology) to which neo-liberalism was a reaction. Toye treats 'left-wing' political economists in rather general terms, and even lumps them together as the exponents of what he calls 'the standard left view' (for example, of the state), even though it is sometimes hard to think of any individual theorist who has actually subscribed to the view he describes; but what is interesting is that Toye seems to be at least as hostile to them as to the neoliberals, and this draws attention to the fact that the ground Toye sees himself occupying is the sensible, reasonable, middle ground, in between these untenable extremes. What is the nature of this terrain?

The answer is not immediately obvious. Toye is a careful and penetrating critic of other theories, but the standpoint from which his criticism is made is not so clear. For instance, he explicitly subscribes to the following views, among others: 'global modernization' is 'inherently conflictual' because it is 'a human directed historical process' (p. 6); what is practicable and desirable is 'managed capitalism' (p. 10); in seeking to promote development we must avoid bringing preconceptions from outside, and see things through the eyes of poor people in the countries concerned (p. 40); and the recent economic retrogression in so much of the Third World 'appears to be a short-period interruption to a long period of buoyant growth' (p. 34).

Now, none of these ideas is self-evident. Why should human-directed historical processes be considered inherently conflictual, rather than inherently collaborative? What theory of history or human nature is involved here? On what grounds does it make sense to believe in 'managed capitalism' as an ideal, given capital's dramatically successful escape from management into the realm of the 'self-regulating' global market since the 1970s? On what grounds and in what circumstances are the perceptions of poor people to be respected, relative to other kinds of understanding? (What makes their thinking about economics important or valid, but not, for example, their ideas about the supernatural?) And from what theoretical standpoint does the retrogression of the last decade or more appear as a short-period interruption to growth, rather than as a long term, if not permanent, reversal?

Toye undoubtedly has answers to such questions. What is interesting is that he does not seem to feel the need to offer them; he does not defend his assumptions, eclectic and open to challenge as they are. He attacks both the left and the right for being teleological, for theorizing development as 'the gradual movement to a single desired social state', calling instead for a 'modest', 'realistic' acceptance of diversity and of the ultimate unpredictability of events (pp. 14-16). This may sound sensible; it undoubtedly makes it easier for the business of the development community to continue at a time when a more demanding canon of theoretical coherence would make it more difficult.

Or a more demanding conception of development as a goal. For it is also worth reflecting on what Toye puts in place of the 'single desired social state' (another straw man – who on the right or the left has really advocated this?) that he rejects as a 'teleological' approach to development: 'what most people would say mattered ultimately', he suggests, 'is the ending of large-scale poverty... sickness, ignorance and premature death, not to mention the violence, ugliness and despair of daily life' (p. 36). Apart from the fact that this seems no less 'teleological' than any other goal of development, where do these values come from? Who are these 'most people' whose authority is being appealed to here, and who no longer care about equality or democracy? Is this 'common sense', in whose name theory, left and right, is attacked, anything other than the tradition of Western charity?

Dependency theory in the 1990s

Dependency theory in its early sense of a general theory that sought to explain underdevelopment at the periphery as almost wholly the insuperably self-perpetuating effect of metropolitan capital probably has few remaining adherents. The NICs showed that structures of dependence might sometimes be overcome, while growing interdependence among even industrialized economies has made all dependence relative. However, dependency theory's focus on the many forms of acute dependence of small, open, ex-colonial economies on the powerful economic interests and states that dominate the financial and commodity markets in which they operate ('concrete situations of dependency') remains indisputably valid. In this primarily heuristic sense of the term, dependency theory has passed into the standard conceptual toolkit of most people who seriously study problems of development, and no longer needs or attracts much general exposition.[27] But it is interesting, all the same, to see how the changes that have occurred in the real world were seen by one of dependency theory's most famous Western exponents, the late Andre Gunder Frank, who described the changes in his own thinking in an autobiographical essay published in 1991.[28]

Much of the charm of this memoir lies in its documentation of Frank's successive friendships and quarrels with other development theorists, and its idiosyncratic mix of (probably valid) claims to have been far in advance of general opinion on nearly every issue of development theory, and (no doubt equally valid) admissions to having been wrong (along with later general opinion, of course). What concerns us here, however, is what Frank finished up thinking. On dependency theory, his own summarized auto-critique reads as follows:

1) Real dependence exists, of course, and more than ever despite denials to the contrary. However, dependence 'theory' and policy never answered the question of how to eliminate real dependence and how to pursue the chimera of non- or in-dependent growth. 2) Dependence heterodoxy nonetheless maintained the orthodoxy that (under)development must refer to and be organised by and through (nation state) societies, countries or regions. However this orthodox tenet turns out to be wrong. 3) I turned orthodoxy on its head, but I maintained the essence of the thesis that economic-growth-through-capital-accumulation equals development... Therefore, I precluded any real alternative definitions, policy and praxis of 'development'. 4) In particular, this orthodoxy incorporated the patriarchal gender structure of society as a matter of course. However much I may personally have been against male chauvinism, I thereby prevented examination of this dimension of dependence (p. 37).

Points (1) and (3) are the most telling criticisms made by sympathetic commentators on Frank's work at the time of its greatest currency. Point (4) acknowledges a blind spot which Frank's partner and collaborator Marta Fuentes induced him to recognize. But it is point (2) that was the most significant for the subsequent course of Frank's thinking. What does it mean to say that development is not something for societies, countries or regions to organize?

As the 1970s progressed, Frank, exiled from Chile to England following the coup and the murder of his friend and early protector, President Allende, became convinced that not only was dependency theory devoid of any convincing alternative conception of development, but the whole idea of national development, which had been the raison d'être of development theory, was no longer tenable in the emerging conditions of a worldwide market. His historical work on the emergence of the capitalist world system led him to see all dreams of alternative development paths pursued by particular countries or regions 'delinked' from that system as illusory (a conclusion fortified by the productive as well as moral bankruptcy of 'actually existing socialism'), while his work on the 'crisis' into which the world capitalist system had entered in the 1970s convinced him that for most of the Third World development within the system was also impossible. In particular, so long as Third

World countries were paying on average about 6.5% of their gross national product (GNP) to service their debt, as he estimated was the case through much of the 1980s, there could only be 'development of underdevelopment', with 'disinvestment in productive infrastructure and human capital and with the loss of competitiveness on the world market'.

The theoretical position to which this led Frank was that the only useful object of study is 'world development', which sets the limits to whatever normative goals it makes sense to try to pursue, and that the only useful agents capable of pursuing such goals are 'particular groups or classes'. Such goals, even if they can be achieved by such groups or classes, will be relative to the way world development currently affects the part of the globe they live in, a development that has been going on throughout recorded history:

> I now find the same continuing world system, including its center-periphery structure, hegemony-rivalry competition, and cyclical ups and downs has been evolving (developing?) for five thousand years at least ... In this world system, sectors, regions and peoples temporarily and cyclically assume leading and hegemonic central (core) positions of social and technological 'development'. They then have to cede their pride of place to new ones who replace them. Usually this happens after a long interregnum of crisis in the system. During this time of crisis, there is intense competition for leadership and hegemony. The central core has moved around the globe in a predominantly westerly direction. With some zig-zags, the central core has passed through Asia, East (China), Central (Mongolia), South (India) and West (Iran, Mesopotamia, Egypt, Turkey)... Then the core passed on to Southern and Western Europe and Britain, via the Atlantic to North America, and now across it and the Pacific towards Japan. Who knows, perhaps one day it will pass all the way around the world to China (pp. 56-57).

Development theory based on any idea of 'autonomous' national development, on any conception of 'de-linking', is, therefore, an illusion (p. 58). What is needed is 'a more rounded, dynamic and all-encompassing supply and demand side economics to analyse, if not to guide, world economic and technological development'. The

significance of the words 'if not to guide' was not made clear: perhaps
Frank was still faintly agnostic on the possibility of some form
of world government emerging? But, for any particular country,
region, sector, group or individual, he was very specific: having a
development 'policy' simply means finding 'one or more niches in
which to carve out a temporary position of "comparative" monopoly
advantage in the international division of labour' (p. 57). 'But for
much of Africa, and probably also Bangladesh, the Brazilian north-
east, Central America, the North American rustbelt and much of the
former socialist world, the prospect is only of marginalization and
decline. Most development for one group ... comes at the expense
of anti-development for others. They are condemned to dualistic
marginalisation and/or to underdevelopment of development. That
is what real world development really means' (pp. 58-60). And, since
all existing models of development are inadequate, Frank pinned
his hopes only on radical democratization, based on the emerging
strength of the hitherto neglected social groups, and especially
women.

The pessimism of Frank's conclusion does not ultimately rest
on theoretical grounds, however (any more than does the optimism
of the Washington Post cited earlier). For example, at one time he
was an exponent of regional trading blocs committed to the defence
of shared political and social values – the sort of thing of which the
Social Chapter of the Maastricht Treaty is a pale reflection – but he
seems to have abandoned this idea without giving any reason for
no longer believing in its potential. His loss of faith in the power
of states to achieve anything in present conditions was not argued
for either, even if it is fairly evident that the states of the countries
that most need effective development policies are those least likely
to be able to produce or implement one.

It is to this point, of course, that interpreting the success of the
NICs is so crucially relevant. At one time their success was attributed
by neo-liberals to the virtues of laissez-faire, until the work of
Hamilton, White, Amsden, Wade and others showed incontrovertibly

that, if anything, the NICs' experience demonstrated the precise opposite, i.e. the necessity for forceful, systematic and sustained economic intervention by a strong, centralized state pursuing a coherent long-term development strategy.[29] This conclusion was later swallowed, albeit with some difficulty, by the World Bank;[30] but its implications for 'development theory' have still to be fully digested in 'mainstream' circles.

To see this, it is worth looking briefly at the work of the American political scientist, Stephan Haggard. Haggard did not see himself as a dependency theorist, but he did set out to see what conclusions should be drawn from the experience of the NICs, using the methods of US political science.* Through a comparative study of the recent history of South Korea, Taiwan, Singapore, Hong Kong, Mexico and Brazil, he identified four main causes for their varying degrees of success: first, external pressure for change, in the form of price shocks, reinforced in several cases by great power influence and leverage; second, favourable constellations of political interests, especially a weakened agricultural elite; third, a state with the capacity to formulate coherent and centrally-implemented policies, with suitable policy instruments (financial institutions, fiscal and regulatory regimes, etc.), and a strong degree of political insulation from economically powerful interests; and fourth, technical competence, 'policy-relevant knowledge'. Haggard analysed how each of these conditions, which were present to different extents and in very different forms in the six cases studied, interacted with their varying geographic and resource endowments to make possible the dramatic adjustments involved in the rapid transition to international manufacturing competitiveness.

---

*Besides his useful extension of the analysis to include two Latin American 'NICs', Haggard had a greater impact on US political scientists than Amsden or the writers of the 'Sussex school', which is a further reason for focusing particularly on his work here. Haggard also dissociated himself from the ritual attacks on dependency theory that seemed to become almost a test of soundness for many US political scientists: see Stephan Haggard, *Pathways From the Periphery: The Politics of Growth in the Newly Industrializing Countries* (Ithaca: Cornell University Press, 1990), p. 19.

His conclusions were cautious, but in general very clear: all of these conditions seemed to have been important, if not indispensable, and perhaps above all the combination of consistent policy (even in the case of Hong Kong, which pursued a policy of almost complete laissez-faire) with strong insulation from political pressure from affected sections of society, including powerful agricultural and business interests. While authoritarian rule was clearly not a sufficient condition for competitiveness, Haggard concluded, it may often be a necessary one.

The substantive implication of Haggard's findings seems to be that not many underdeveloped countries are likely to meet the necessary conditions in the foreseeable future. Furthermore, Haggard did not analyse the distinctiveness of the international context at the time of these countries' decisive advances, i.e. how far their development successes depended on such factors as buoyant conditions of world demand, or the exceptionally large capital flows and access to the US market made available by the USA to Korea and Taiwan – factors very unlikely to be replicated elsewhere.

There is, finally, a further theoretical point that needs to be made. Haggard's study offered no grounds for trying to answer the question of how any other country might ever put itself in the position to replicate the NICs' conditions for successful industrialization. His comparative analysis did not extend to the specific histories that produced the relative sophistication of these countries' pre-existing markets, technology and capital stock, the competence of their entrepreneurial classes and state technocracies, the relative autonomy of their state apparatuses and the relative political weakness of their landed and working classes. But for the analysis of the NICs to contribute to a new theory of development these histories are evidently crucial: can we say anything at all general about the processes that each of these countries had to pass through to produce the specific mix of conditions that made its breakthrough possible? What cultural characteristics permitted the formation of the necessary consensus within its state apparatus about the development strategies it adopted, and the necessary technical understanding to implement them consistently and effectively? To answer this kind of question, however, we are forced out of what Bayart calls 'weak ahistorical comparativism' into the study of comparative historical dynamics, i.e. into the kind of enquiry for which there is still no serious alternative to some of the central theoretical ideas of Marx.[31]

Rational choice and development

One of the most influential reactions – at least in the USA – to the end of 'development theory's' raison d'être was to try to build a new political economy of development in which the key to economic performance is seen as institutions that can be analysed in terms of rational choice theory.

This response made sense in several ways. First, it involved going back to the problem raised by Myrdal and his colleagues in the 1960s – how to incorporate the obstacles posed by political and social phenomena into the analysis of economic development – but this time in a way that explicitly tried to stay within the assumptions of neo-classical or marginalist economics: that is, unlike the neo-Weberians of the modernization school (not to mention Marxists or neo-Marxists), the 'new institutionalism' was supposed to rest on the assumption of rational individuals maximizing their utilities and nothing more, and should (in its most optimistic version, at least) be capable of being integrated with economics and modelled mathematically. Given the recent ascendancy of neo-classical economics in the 'development community', this had an air of political realism about it (and maybe – some people evidently hoped – it could also endow political science with some of the economists' famous rigour).

Second, it held out the prospect of dispensing with the Marxist phenomenology of classes and relations of production and other unclean entities, whose relevance to the problems of development cannot always be denied; in the choice-theoretic discourse all of these are reducible to special cases of a very small stock of extremely general concepts, such as institutions, organizations and their principals and agents.

The central idea of the 'new institutionalism' or 'new political economy' is that what makes for an efficient economy is a set of institutions that permit individuals to benefit personally from doing what will also serve the (material) interests of society as a whole. Thus, for instance, a system of land tenure that allows tenants to keep for themselves a significant part of any expanded output they produce through allocating extra resources of capital or effort to its production is more economically efficient than one which does not. This reasoning can be applied to taxation, the organization of central or local government, education, banking, marketing – in effect, to any social arrangements (even marriage law and custom). Conversely it is often possible to see, retrospectively, that the institutional structure has provided incentives for individuals to do things which were inimical to development; while prospectively it is often possible to imagine or even design institutional arrangements that will improve the social returns to the economic activity of individuals (which is, roughly, what management consultants are supposed to be concerned with when they are hired by the state).

But in the absence of further arguments this does not amount to a theory of development, or even a significant addition to existing theories, for a very simple but fundamental reason: we cannot explain in terms of the 'paradigm' how any particular set of institutions that existed in the past or exist today in a given country came into existence. For that we have to resort to a much wider, looser theory of social change of precisely the kind that most exponents of public choice theory are trying to dispense with. Douglass North, who can fairly claim to be the chief inspirer of the idea that choice-theoretic thinking can yield a new theory of development, is strikingly ambivalent on this point. On the one hand, he is clear that

> Neoclassical economics ... may account very well for the performance
> of an economy at a moment of time or, with comparative statistics,
> contrasts in the performance of an economy over time; but it does
> not and cannot explain the dynamics of change. The major source
> of changes in an economy over time is structural change in the
> parameters held constant by the economist – technology, population,
> property rights, and government control over resources. Changes in
> political-economic organisation and its consequent effects are basic
> to theorising about all these sources of structural change.[32]

And he even adds that 'the Marxian theory is the most powerful of the existing statements of secular change precisely because it includes all of the elements left out of the neoclassical framework: institutions, property rights, the state, and ideology' – even though he thinks the Marxian theory has various faults and is, at best, a special case of change and unacceptable as a general theory.

On the other hand, he thinks that changes in institutions (which on his definition include property rights and the state) can be incorporated into neo-classical analysis through the concept of a 'path' of change that flows from the interaction between the existing institutions and the organizations that individuals form to maximize their utilities within the framework of incentives offered by the institutions. This interaction leads to modifications of the institutions over time, typically in an incremental way that tends to reinforce whatever tendency the original institutions had to be socially efficient or inefficient; this is roughly what is meant by the 'path dependency' of a social system in this parlance. Once an adequate inventory of a country's existing institutions and organizations has been made, then, it should be possible to infer the development path that it will follow as a result of their interaction; even the modifications that are likely to be made to the institutions, and hence the subsequent changes in organizational behaviour, should be deducible. In other words, a general development theory of the kind Marx proposed, but capable of being integrated with neo-classical economics, should be within our grasp.

There are, however, three basic difficulties with this idea. First, the concept of 'ideology' has to be expanded to deal with everything that cannot be included within the assumptions of choice theory. North is quite aware of the fact that he must rely on 'ideology' to deal with such problems as historically-decisive instances of collective behaviour which on strict individual utility-maximizing assumptions should not have occurred because of the 'free-rider problem' (i.e. they should not have been possible because it would have been in everyone's best individual interest to leave it to others to run the risks and pay the price involved); and so he calls for a theory of ideology to complement the theory of institutions.[33]

But it is not clear that he recognizes how fatal this is to his project. So much of the problem of understanding social change is understanding what motivates collective action, and the results of centuries of study and reflection suggest very strongly that there are not going to be any general, or any simple, answers. Any interesting answers have always been specific to historically well-studied places and times (such as the French Revolution, or the nineteenth century labour movement in Europe), and have involved complex long-term and short-term interactions between individuals, groups, cultural practices and institutions of specific kinds (churches, constitutions, professions, communities, armies) – in short, they almost always involve the social whole, including many of the very things ('institutions') which for North's project must be kept analytically separate from 'ideology'.

A second difficulty is the project's reductionism. For instance, the idea that developmentally significant change may be understood as being the result of the interaction between existing institutions and the organizations formed to achieve whatever goals the institutional structure makes possible and attractive is, obviously, a very general statement about the sort of relationship that Marx postulated between classes and property rights. Presumably the advantage of reformulating it in these terms is that it brings out the general characteristics, which any such hypothesis needs to have, in a way that does not prejudge what it will actually state. The difficulty is, however, that whatever plausibility the general statement has comes from the particular case, not from the abstract one, which looks like a tautology. In effect, North is stating that any theory that is to replace Marx's needs to be of this general character. But, in so far as this is true, it is not new, and, in so far as it is new, it is not obviously true. In so far as it is true, few Marxists today would disagree that we need a theory of Marx's kind, but better; the problem is only to have the learning and analytic power to come up with one. But, if the suggestion is that we need a theory that can be formulated entirely within the assumptions of rational choice theory, its truth is by no means obvious. That idea comes from a preference for rational choice theory based on meta-theoretical grounds, not because it has been shown to be suitable for handling large-scale and long-term social change, since (as North himself notes) this is not the case.

Third, there is a closely related tendency, even in North's thinking (which is in general sensitive to such problems), to argue that, because some aspect of observed reality can be modelled, that aspect is the determinative or key one. For instance, institutions are very broadly defined, in this literature, as systems of rules or norms constraining behaviour, which means that virtually all persisting social relations can be represented as institutions.[34] But then the claim that institutions 'are the underlying determinant of the long-run performance of economies' becomes an unhelpful truism – i.e. the pattern of social relations determines economic performance.[35] Yet when North makes this claim it does not feel like a truism. This is because by this time he has built a rational choice model of certain aspects of institutions having to do with property rights and their related transaction costs, incentive structures and so on, which have obvious economic implications.

But what about the determinative effects of all the other aspects of all the other kinds of institutions not susceptible of being modelled in this way? What about the effects of the passions aroused in religious movements, or the conservatism, loyalty, discipline, etc., embodied in cultural norms, or the reforming or revolutionary zeal generated by class or national feeling, all of which seem to have played no less crucial parts in determining economic performance at one time or another in history? They can be brought back in only by accepting that the claim that institutions are the 'underlying' determinant is true by definition. It is plausible that, other things being held constant, property laws will have important effects on economic performance. But the whole difficulty of understanding development, as North frequently acknowledges, is that other things do not stay constant but continually interact with property rights and all other kinds of social relations in ways that cannot be comprised within any model as simple and one-sided as those of rational choice theorizing.

Thus, while rational choice undoubtedly has valuable contributions to make to specific issues in development – the work of Samuel Popkin on peasant farmers' behaviour is an excellent example – it does not point the way towards a new development theory for our times.

'Rethinking Third World politics'

Assuming, that is, that we are still concerned with development. The response of some academics was, on the contrary, to frankly abandon it. Thus James Manor wrote in the introduction to *Rethinking Third World Politics* that he and his fellow contributors were

> not interested... in influencing the countries we are studying. We do not even intend these studies to advance the cause of democracy in theThirdWorld, even though we wish it well. We believe that that cause is best served by studies which provide the most sophisticated possible understanding of how things actually work in Third World political systems.[36]

Leaving aside the question of how research that appears to deny its own value commitments could be sophisticated, it is interesting to see what is involved in abandoning any policy concerns, including any commitment to 'development', by examining the work of the most fertile and wide-ranging of Manor's contributors, Jean-François Bayart.

In his chapter entitled 'Finishing with the Idea of the Third World: The Concept of the Political Trajectory', Bayart outlines his concept of 'historicity', the idea that politics must always be understood as a moment in a complex and very long-term story. This story can be understood, Bayart suggests, in three possible ways: as the story of a 'civilization' (in Braudel's sense), as the story of a system of inequalities (caste, class, age, etc.), or as the story of a culture – or as a combination of these. Out of people's experience of this past, or these pasts – pasts which, Bayart stresses, comprise external influences as well as forces endogenous to the country or region under study – they have constructed various 'discursive genres', in terms of which politics are understood: examples he gives include such widely differing genres of discourse as the British system of government (a discourse about representation, civil liberties, etc.), Islamic thought, and the 'world of the invisible' (the occult, witchcraft, etc.). People think in terms of these discourses, and politics are constrained by them while at the same time involving contestations between them. The analysis of politics must therefore, according to Bayart, try to link 'the collective work of the production of the state to the subjective interiority of its actors' (p. 68) by studying both the long-term historicity of a people, through which their political institutions have evolved, and the discourses through which these institutions are participated in and understood today.

These statements are programmatic. To assess their practical significance we can take Bayart's major study, *The State in Africa*, as a case in point.[37] In this book his stated purpose is to understand the 'historicity' of the African post-colonial state. He wants to transcend the shorter-term theories of the 'developmentalists', the 'modernization' school, the dependency school, 'the Marxists' and various others – all of whom share, in his view, more or less the same basic error: i.e. they ignore, or radically misunderstand, Africa's 'true historicity' (p. 5).

In contrast, Bayart offers a 'longue durée' view of Africans as having over the centuries always been subordinate players in relation to the outside world, but players none the less, always engaged in a process of 'extraversion', in which they have sought to draw on resources or alliances available in the external environment in furtherance of their continuing internal competitions and conflicts. What we have now is only the latest version of this role, although now enacted on wider stages than in earlier times – in the ex-colonial territories, and in a number of regional 'power-spaces' (West, East and Southern Africa, polarized around Nigeria-Zaire, Kenya and South Africa respectively). What is now going on, Bayart argues, is the construction of new historic blocs, 'rhizomatically' linked to the underlying societies (i.e. like shoots from a tuber) and clustering around the state, and actually combining elements that earlier theorists have tended to see as mutually exclusive and opposed to each other: traditional and modern elites, local and central elites, chiefs and civil servants, state and private-sector elites, etc. In Bayart's view, ethnicity, class and the rest are all interlinked in a 'reciprocal assimilation of elites', as the members of these elites collaborate with each other to profit as best they can from their dealings with the world outside.

And so what earlier theorists saw as deformations or aberrations appear in Bayart's optic as more or less normal, and in truth functional. Even a deeply corrupt state can be seen as an integrative force; even military coups can be understood as modes of intervention to cool out elite competition which has become out of control and destabilizing (p. 154); even structural adjustment programmes may be seen as removing spoils from the control of parts of the historic bloc that the president might otherwise not be able to dominate adequately (pp. 225-26). Bayart does not paint the post-colonial African state in rosy colours: the sick brutality of a Bokassa in the Central African Republic, a Touré in Guinea or an

Eyedama in Togo is spelled out. But this kind of sadistic violence is seen as exceptional, while the colossal predations of less vicious rulers appear as essentially inevitable, inscribed in the continent's 'historicity'.

As for the African masses, Bayart frequently asserts that they are not passive victims of external forces, that they make their own history; but the actual role he shows them playing is circumscribed so closely by their lack of capacity to act for themselves, and by their desperate struggle for survival, that they more often seem carried along by the trends he describes. At one point (p. 259) he even presents refugees as a kind of heroes ('escapees'), demonstrating the limitations of the power of state power-holders by exercising the 'exit option'; and yet in their very act of leaving Bayart also seems to make them responsible for the shortcomings of the situation they leave behind – their absence contributes to the weakness of civil society, the lack of capital accumulation, and hence to the existence of only a thieving, rather than a productive, ruling elite!

In the same passage, it is true, Bayart also characterizes refugees as 'unfortunate crowds hurrying towards frontiers and vegetating in reception camps'. But what, from the standpoint of the longue durée, is unfortunate about these crowds? For there is notable inconsistency in Bayart's account, in its oscillation between a sort of gruff realism about the post-colonial state, and moral discomfort. For where the modernization school expected the African elites to be modernizing and good, Bayart expects them to be interested in power, wealth and status at more or less any cost. His standpoint might seem Hegelian: history unfolds according to the cunning of reason, so that it makes no sense to shed tears for history's victims. To do so is inconsistent, and furthermore empty, since there is no way to intervene. But, unlike Hegel, Bayart does not subscribe to an 'objective idealism'. In his concept of history there is no higher purpose which people's suffering serves.

And this is what it means to try to study the Third World without any commitment. The work of those committed to 'development' had faults, but thanks to this commitment they all had some idea – however imperfect – of who they were writing for, and who might act in the light of what they wrote. Bayart's intended readers, on the other hand, seem to be ultimately just 'Africanists', capable of getting their minds round Africa's 'historicity', but with neither the power nor the wish to act historically. As with Toye's stance, this may have an air of being more 'realistic' than the stance of Marxists, dependency theorists or modernizers, but what does this amount to?

Bayart has evident affinities with post-structuralist discourse, according to which we can never know reality but can only make a variety of statements about it with varying degrees and kinds of usefulness. Among social scientists a frequent symptom of this idea is to lay stress on the complexity of everything and the way no one formulation ever fully captures it, a 'distancing effect' that certainly seems to play a part in Bayart's work. But, even within that discourse, something eventually is said, a choice of statements is made, a general account emerges. And then, it is fair to ask, from what standpoint is Bayart's ultimately quietist picture drawn? And for whom is it painted, if not for the aforementioned kleptocrats, whom it does not exactly celebrate, but does not condemn either?

Consistently, for someone uncommitted to any concept of development, Bayart makes a resolute separation of politics from economics and says virtually nothing about the relation between them. In his account of Africa, what matters is only how economic resources are appropriated to service the endless cycle of the reciprocal assimilation of elites. If at the end of the twentieth century many African countries were destined to suffer desertification, famine, crime and warlordism, or to undergo recolonization as vast refugee camps, is it of great importance in the longue durée? In practice, Bayart has been an active spokesman for African interests in French public debate. The stance outside or above the fray that he explicitly adopts in his thesis on historicity contradicts this, and it is this contradiction that repeatedly surfaces in these texts.

In conclusion: development, or the fate of the ancients?

These sketches of a few selected currents in contemporary writing about development (or, in the case of Manor and Bayart, in reaction against development) are, of course, subjective and partial. Their point is to raise the question of what 'development theory' was and has become, and above all to try to clarify what seems to me to be at stake: namely, the urgent need to revive development theory, not as a branch of policy-orientated social science within the parameters of an unquestioned capitalist world order, but as a field of critical enquiry about the contemporary dynamics of that order itself, with imperative policy implications for the survival of civilized and decent life, and not just in the ex-colonial countries.

Since the late 1960s, the debate about 'development theory' has in fact been more and more clearly about the theory of global development that each one presupposed, although the participants all too often did not recognize, or did not acknowledge, that this was the issue at stake. Today it has to be frankly confronted: what do 'the universal development of the productive forces' and a truly global relation of supply and demand, which the OECD governments and the international financial institutions have been labouring for more than three decades to realize, now imply for any individual project of 'development'? For whom, contemplating what goals and by what means, can a useful 'development theory' be constructed?

The scale on which these questions seem to oblige us to think is painfully vast, and may seem almost to threaten incoherence; but, if it was not impossible to have a theory of capitalism on a national scale, why should it be impossible to have one of capitalism on a global scale? The theories of Hegel or Marx (or Weber or Fukuyama, for that matter) are not incoherent, but just very large-scale and necessarily full of selective simplifications, speculative elements, debatable assumptions and 'middle-level' problems of all kinds. What is really incoherent is a 'devlopment theory' that does not rest explicitly on as clear a general theory of world history, and of world capitalism in particular, as it is possible to have.

Such a theory must, evidently, indicate what is and is not possible for various potential actors, just as the Keynesian theory of global capitalism did at the birth of 'development theory'. On the basis of such a general theory, new development theories at a lower level of abstraction can then be formulated. These may be for states, for groups of states organized in regional or other organizations or for non-state agents of various kinds. The goals of development envisaged by these theories will depend on the actors for whom they are formulated and the scope for change that the theorist's preferred theory of world capitalism suggests exists for them. If, as I fear, it seems that not much scope for change exists – especially for small, severely underdeveloped countries – without a radical resubordination of capital to democratic control, development theory will have also to be about this, and agents capable of undertaking it.

This abstract conclusion seems to me preferable, in spite of its abstraction, to trying to breathe life back into any kind of 'development theory' whose illusory appearance of concreteness and 'practicality' depends on averting one's gaze from its lack of adequate foundations.

Endnotes

1   'Philosophy of Right and Law', in Carl J. Friedrich (ed.), *The Philosophy of Hegel* (New York: Random House, 1953), p. 227.

2   'The German Ideology', in Robert Tucker (ed.), *The Marx-Engels Reader* (New York: W.W. Norton, second edition 1978), pp. 161-62.

3   See the neat resumé of this in Francis Fukuyama, *The End of History and the Last Man* (New York: The Free Press, 1992), Chapter 5.

4   G.W.F. Hegel, 'The Philosophy of History', in Friedrich (ed.), *The Philosophy of Hegel*, op. cit., p. 11 and passim; he concludes (p. 23):

'World history presents therefore the stages of the principle whose meaning is the consciousness of freedom.'

5 Karl Marx, 'Introduction' to the Grundrisse, in Tucker (ed.), *The Marx-Engels Reader*, op. cit., p. 241.

6 W.W. Rostow, *The Stages of Economic Growth: A Non-Communist Manifesto* (Cambridge: Cambridge University Press, 1960).

7 An outstanding contribution to the study of development theory as discourse is David B. Moore and Gerald G. Schmitz (eds.), *Debating Development Discourse: Institutional and Popular Perspectives* (London: Macmillan, 1994); see especially the penetrating and rich opening chapter by Moore, 'Development Discourse as Hegemony: Towards an Ideological History – 1945-1995', pp. 1-29. Moore's position is at many points similar to, and has also influenced, my own. Moore focuses primarily on development theory's role in the struggle for international hegemony. While this dimension is politically crucial it seems to me likely that on further investigation the professional and organizational dimensions of development discourses (some of the elements of which are outlined in his chapter) will acquire more salience.

8 P.W. Preston, *Theories of Development* (London: Routledge, 1982), Chapter 3, referring to the work of Harrod and Domar and their successors, 'exported' to the soon-to-be ex-colonies.

9 Gunnar Myrdal, *Asian Drama: An Enquiry Into the Poverty of Nations* (NewYork: TheTwentieth Century Fund, 1968), Vol. I, p. 66. See also Chapter 18, sections 13-14.

10 Irene Gendzier, *Managing Political Change: Social Scientists and the Third World* (Boulder: Westview, 1985). This is a central text for any serious understanding of the genesis of American development theory in US foreign policy and anticommunism. The leading exponents of the political development sub-field of modernization theory listed by Gendzier are Gabriel Almond, David Apter, Leonard Binder, James S. Coleman, Karl Deutsch, S.N. Eisenstadt, Samuel P. Huntington, Joseph LaPalombara, Harold D. Lasswell, Daniel Lerner, Max Millikan, Lucien Pye, Edward A. Shils, Sidney Verba and Myron Weiner. American critics of their views were few and far between.

11 For Frank's intellectual itinerary see his 'The Underdevelopment of Development', special issue of the *Scandinavian Journal of Development Alternatives* 10/3, September 1991.

12 This was the most telling theoretical criticism in Bill Warren's influential article, 'Imperialism and Capitalist Industrialisation', *New Left Review* 81, 1973, pp.3-44. The definitive discussion of this point is in Gavin Kitching, *Development and Underdevelopment in Historical Perspective* (London: Methuen, 1982).

13 F.H. Cardoso, 'Dependency and Development in Latin America', *New Left Review* 74, 1972, pp. 83-95.

14 The conclusions of Jorge Larrain on this point cannot be improved upon: 'There is little doubt that if one examines the theory of dependency... as a testable theory with precisely defined variables and concepts whose characteristics are exclusive and apply only to dependent countries and one requiring measurable empirical evidence which substantiates the hypotheses, then the theory of dependency does not seem to pass the test... But one wonders whether this attempt to judge the theory of dependence in accordance with such a formal pattern is really worthwhile. Such an attempt is bound to abstract from and miss what had been the essence of the theory in its origins and in the intention of its best representatives: the historical analysis of Latin American processes "as the result of struggles between classes and groups that define their interests and values in the process of expansion of a mode of production" and which "in the struggle for control or for the reformulation of the existing order... are making a given structure of domination historically viable or are transforming it." (Jorge Larrain, citing Cardoso, in Larrain, *Theories of Development: Capitalism, Colonialism and Dependency* [Oxford: Polity Press, 1989], pp. 178-79).

15 'The radical critics of orthodox development theory were so keen to prove the ideological point that underdevelopment was the product of capitalist exploitation, that they let the crucial issue pass them by: capital created underdevelopment not because it exploited the underdeveloped world, but because it did not exploit it enough' (Geoffrey Kay, *Development and Underdevelopment: A Marxist Analysis* [London: Macmillan, 1975], p. x).

16 Radhika Desai, 'Second Hand Dealers in Ideas: Think Tanks and Thatcherite Hegemony', *New Left Review* 203, 1994, pp. 27-64.

17 *Dilemmas of Development: Reflections on the Counter-revolution in Development Economics* (Oxford: Basil Blackwell, second edition 1993), p. 143. Dependency theorists, in contrast, had from the first emphasized the tendency of Third World elites in power to serve their

own and foreigners' interests at the expense of their people's collective interests. Unlike the neo-liberals, on the other hand, they did not make the mistake of assuming that no Third World governments were ever genuinely concerned for the public interest.

18 *World Development Report 1991*, p. 18.

19 Manfred Bienefeld, Rescuing the Dream of Development in the Nineties, Silver Jubilee Paper 10 (University of Sussex: Institute of Development Studies, 1991, p. 13): a terse and powerful critique of the course and effects of structural adjustment policies.

20 Glyn and Sutcliffe, 'Global But Leaderless? The New Capitalist Order', in the *Socialist Register 1992*, (London: Merlin Press, 1992), pp. 90-91.

21 'A World Growing Richer', Washington Post editorial in the Manchester Guardian, ~ekry, 26 June 1994. The editorial adds: 'The countries that have been left out of this surge fall mainly into two categories: the ones that have been entangled in long wars, and most of those in America.' The USA's role in these wars, and in the arms trade, is not mentioned in the editorial.

22 'The Underdevelopment of Development', op. cit., pp. 48-49. The situation is not essentially different in the industrialized countries, as Susan Strange remarks in *Casino Capitalism* (Oxford: Blackwell, 1987, p. 3): 'Political leaders and their opponents like to pretend that they are still in control of their national economies ... But recent years have shown again and again how the politicians' plans have been upset by changes that they could not have foreseen in the world outside the state'. See chapter 2, below.

23 'Development Economics in the 1950s', in Meier and Seers (eds.), *Pioneers in Development*, p. 137.

24 Frans J. Schuurman (ed.), *Beyond the Impasse: New Directions in Development Theory* (London: Zed Books, 1993).

25 David Booth, 'Marxism and Development Sociology: Interpreting the Impasse', *World Development* 13/7, 1985, pp. 761-87; see also, among others, Peter Vandergeest and Frederick H. Buttell, 'Marx, Weber and Development Sociology: Beyond the Impasse', and Leslie Sklair, 'Transcending the Impasse: Metatheory, Theory, and Empirical Research in the Sociology of Underdevelopment', both in *World Development* 16/6, 1988, pp. 683-95 and 697-709.

26 *Dilemmas of Development*, op. cit.

27 An exemplary exposition of dependency thinking as a central dimension of the analysis of the impact of global market forces on the periphery is to be found in a long series of influential papers by Manfred Bienefeld, some of which have already been cited. Others include, notably, 'Dependency in the Eighties', *IDS Bulletin* 12/2, 1980, pp. 5-10; 'The International Context for National Development Strategies: Constraints and Opportunities in a Changing World', in Manfred Bienefeld and Godfrey Martin (eds.), *The Struggle for Development: National Strategies in an International Context* (Chichester: Wiley, 1982); 'The Significance of the Newly Industrialising Countries for the Development Debate', *Studies in Political Economy*, 25, Spring 1988, pp. 7-39; and 'Structural Adjustment: Debt Collection Device or Development Policy?', *ADMT Series* No.5 (Institute of Comparative Culture, Sophia University, Japan, 1993).

28 'The Underdevelopment of Development', op. cit. (see note 11).

29 See Clive Hamilton, *Capitalist Industrialisation in Korea* (Boulder: Westview, 1986); Gordon White, *Developmental States in East Asia* (New York: St Martin's Press, 1987); Alice Amsden, *Asia's Next Giant: South Korea and Late Industrialization* (New York: Oxford University Press, 1989); and Robert Wade, *Governing the Market: Economic Theory and the Role of Government in East Asian Industrialization* (Princeton: Princeton University Press, 1990).

30 *The East Asian Miracle: Economic Growth and Public Policy* (New York: Oxford University Press for the World Bank, 1993).

31 Jean-François Bayart, 'Finishing with the Idea of the Third World: The Concept of the Political Trajectory', in James Manor (ed.) *Rethinking Third World Politics* (London: Longman, 1991), pp. 53-54.

32 Douglass C. North, *Structure and Change in Economic History* (New York: W.W. Norton, 1981), p. 57.

33 Ibid., p. 107.

34 'Institutions are the rules of the game in a society, or, more formally, are the humanly devised constraints that shape human interaction' (*North, Institutional Change and Economic Performance* [Cambridge: Cambridge University Press, 1990], p. 3).

35 Ibid., p. 107.

36　James Manor (ed.), *Rethinking Third World Politics,* op. cit., p. 2.

37　Jean-François Bayart, *The State in Africa: The Politics of the Belly* (London: Longman, 1993).

Neo-Liberal Democracy

By now, at least, it is a truth generally acknowledged that the abolition of capital controls in the 1980s, leaving capital free to cross national borders, means that national governments can influence their domestic economies only by adopting measures that are seen as market-friendly by increasingly globalised capital markets. But it is much less widely acknowledged that all national politics are now market-driven, in a way that has radically changed the meaning of 'democracy'. It is not just that governments can no longer 'manage' their national economies; to survive in office they must increasingly manage national politics in such a way as to adapt them to the pressures of trans-national market forces. These pressures include not only demands for tight constraints on macro-economic policy and favourable regulatory arrangements for investors, but also the direct impact of global economic forces in various economic sectors.

Many of the policies governments are now obliged to adopt in response to these pressures, such as cutting taxes and social security benefits, are inherently unpopular, leading to the politics of 'triangulation' and spin, and the proclamation of 'third ways' through which the contradiction between social needs and the interests of globalised capital is supposed to be miraculously dissolved. On the other hand the continuous deep reshaping of social relations and ideas on business lines by global market forces progressively reduces the public's ability and inclination to resist. The reality of 'liberal democracy' was already a severely constricted concept of democracy; neo-liberal democracy reduces it dangerously close to vanishing-point. If this judgement seems over-stated, the rest of this essay aims to substantiate it.

What is novel about the global economy that took shape after the Second World War, compared with the years before 1914, is, first, the much wider choice of locations for capital investment which capital's new freedom of movement enabled it to choose from; second, the weight and omnipresence of global financial markets; and third, the importance of transnational manufacturing and service corporations, and the advanced communications technology on which they depend. Taken together these features of globalisation mean that capital mobility has not just removed the 'Keynesian capacity' of national governments – their ability to influence the general level of demand; it has made all policy-making sensitive to 'market sentiment' and the regulatory demands of transnational corporations. Governments can try to reduce these pressures through various kinds of protectionism, through participating in global or regional institutions to regulate market forces, and through shedding responsibilities downwards (devolution and 'subsidiarity'), but they can't escape them. States are put under constant pressure to become more and more 'internationalised', adapted to meeting the needs of global market forces. They are also under pressure to restructure themselves on business lines. The old Weberian concept of the independent state official gives way to one modelled on the corporate executive, and not just the implementation of state policy, but state policy-making itself, is increasingly outsourced to private 'consultants'.

How big a change this reversal of power involves for any particular country depends on what existed before. Britain and India, for example, not to mention the USA, have never had market-coordinating, trust-based institutions of the 'Rhineland', 'Nordic' or 'East Asian' types – banks with long-term equity in companies, state-backed national training systems, or 'families' of corporations doing business with each other like the Japanese keiretsu or South Korean chaebols – through which the economic restructuring necessitated by globalisation could be undertaken. Instead the British government actively promoted global capital mobility with a view to exposing the economy as much as possible to global market forces, and entering frankly into competitive deregulation to attract investment. In Britain, too (and much more than in India so far), state institutions have also been radically restructured, with four main aims: to make the state serve business interests; to privatise state-owned enterprises and premises, and the provision of a vast range of public services; to remodel its internal operations on business lines; and to reduce the government's exposure to political pressures from the electorate. The 'Atlanticist' political culture of Britain's political elite may have made them readier than others to pursue this policy, but no country is immune to the pressures to do so. And in all cases, the policy response has profound knock-on effects on society and politics.

The historical context is also a key determinant. In Britain, when the Labour Party finally returned to office in 1997, after 18 years in opposition, the institutional legacy of Thatcherism had gained general acceptance (if little affection) as a result of accompanying social changes – rapid income growth, consumerism, the erosion of traditional class and caste boundaries, the intense 'mediatisation' of politics and the penetration of everyday life by commercial values. The working class voters in Labour's traditional 'heartlands' were now a minority. They could only be helped, Labour's 'modernisers' reasoned, on taking control of the party in 1994, if Labour formed a long-term coalition with capital and secured the approval of the markets – a process which they hoped would also attach middle-class voters permanently to the party. To be able to do these things the party leadership needed to insulate itself from pressures from its own members. The party constitution was rewritten and the

Leader's inner circle assumed unprecedented control over not only the making of policy, but also its day-to-day interpretation.*

The implications of this radical shift in accountability, from party members and voters to the capital markets and global corporations, are most readily seen in the realm of public services such as health services, social services, education and public broadcasting, to which people are attached historically, and as citizens rather than consumers. These domains become political flashpoints because they also are prime targets for takeover by global capital, seeking to convert them from universal services provided out of tax revenues, to commodities sold like any other, from which profits can be made. The outright privatisation of some public services, the outsourcing of the provision of others to private service providers, and the reshaping of government itself on business lines, has proceeded, at varying tempos, everywhere. It turns out that states are by no means impotent, but they increasingly use their power to *advance* the process of commodification of the public realm, rather than resist it. Understanding how this conversion of the state from a protector of national society to an agent of international capital comes about, and what it means for the future, has become the most important task confronting political science – even if (for reasons touched on in the following essay) fewer political scientists than ever seem inclined to undertake it.

The task involved has certainly become more complex. The main causal links no longer converge conveniently in the national capital (whether London, New Delhi or Stockholm) but run off the edge of the national map to Washington, Brussels, the stock exchanges in New York and Tokyo, commodity markets like Chicago's and tax havens like the Bahamas. Bringing out the connections between

---

* And after the Conservatives' defeat in 1997 they tried unsuccessfully to follow Labour's example. In 2006, three leaders later, the party was still struggling with this problem, as its cadre of rank and file members – increasingly consisting of die-hards from an earlier generation – was less acquiescent than Labour's. But their eventual return to power depended on overcoming this resistance.

seemingly (though not really) remote market forces and the changes occurring in people's everyday lives is harder work than it was when a great deal of effective power over the national economy still rested with national governments. On the other hand it is more important than ever to undertake this work. Otherwise cause and effect are dangerously confused. Foreigners are blamed for 'taking away' jobs when job losses are a normal consequence of technological change and raiding under globalised capitalist production. 'Brussels' is blamed for 'taking away British sovereignty', and 'Washington' is blamed for taking away India's, when the sovereignty of both has been much more extensively surrendered to global capital. If we are to reassert our collective needs against the interests and logic of global capital it is essential to understand the way national politics and global market forces are now connected.

The term ⸢market-driven politics⸥ refers simply to the political dimension of the shift of power from voters to capital that results from trans-border capital mobility. It has some affinity with Karl Polanyi's term 'market society', which he coined to refer to a society in which market forces, i.e. capital, had escaped political control (Polanyi had the colonies particularly in mind, and perhaps especially the horrors perpetrated in King Leopold's Congo). 'Market society' was actually inconceivable, Polanyi thought, in any society where the government depended to any degree on popular consent, because it subordinated human welfare and the environment itself to the drive for profit:

> To allow the market mechanism to be the sole director of the fate of human beings and their natural environment, indeed, even of the amount and use of purchasing power, would result in the demolition of society... Robbed of the protective covering of cultural institutions, human beings would perish from the effects of social exposure; they would die as the victims of acute social dislocation through vice, perversion, crime and starvation. Nature would be reduced to its elements, neighbourhoods and landscapes defiled, rivers polluted, military safety jeopardised, the power to produce food and raw materials destroyed.[1]

In 1944, when Polanyi published *The Great Transformation*, he evidently believed that the two most destructive wars in human history had shown that the social costs of allowing capital to escape from political control were too great ever to be risked again. By the late 1970s, however, after three decades of prosperity, people in the North, at least, had forgotten the costs of 'deregulation' and voted for a new instalment of it. We are now starting to measure the costs once again, including the erosion of the social security apparatuses that previous generations fought so long and hard to create. But now that party politics and state policy-making are themselves powerfully market-driven they are less and less likely to defend, let alone renew and revitalise, this crucial prerequisite of genuine democracy – or to confront the world's ultimately greatest challenge, irreversible climate change. We need to understand this, in order to develop an effective alternative politics.

Global market forces
By 1990 a new global economy clearly existed. Production could take place almost anywhere, capital could be invested more or less anywhere, profits could be remitted from more or less anywhere. This did not mean there was a single, homogeneous world-wide market, or that foreign capital could be invested, or foreign goods sold, as easily in Russia or Japan as in Canada. Non-tariff barriers of all kinds remained, and distinctive national tastes did not change overnight, although international sales of US-made films and television programmes, and the penetration of foreign markets by firms like Toyota and MacDonalds, were undoubtedly homogenising tastes to an unprecedented extent, while advances in production technology had made it much easier to vary the product to suit particular regional or even national 'niches' in the world market. As Eric Hobsbawm put it, 'for many purposes, notably in economic affairs, the globe is now the primary operational unit and older units such as "national economies"... are reduced to complications of transnational activities.'[2]

The most significant post-1945 innovations in the global economy are the scale and power of contemporary global financial markets, and the global production and marketing of goods and services by trans-national corporations.

By the end of the 1980s 'deregulation' and computerisation had resulted in the elimination of the most significant geographic barriers to all kinds of financial activity. Besides the phenomenal growth of the currency markets, the securities and bond markets had also been globalized; shares in companies in Japan could be traded as easily in Frankfurt as in Tokyo, and bonds issued by Volkswagen or the city of New York could easily be bought in London. When the London stock exchange closed in the evening, the New York exchange was already open, and when it closed, Tokyo took over until London opened again.* Although there were some important hold-outs against completely free capital movements, including India and China, speaking generally the owners of capital were now free to move it more or less anywhere; and through satellite-based information technology they were also acquiring the capacity to evaluate rapidly more and more alternative ways of investing or banking it world-wide. Net international bank loans rose from 0.7 per cent of world output in 1964 to 16.3 per cent in 1991; bond issues grew at about three times the rate of world output between 1973 and 1995; the volume of derivatives – tradable instruments designed to hedge against risks, especially fluctuating exchange rates, but in the process, taken together, heightening risk – expanded 'astronomically', to a total value in 1996 of $321 trillion, more than the total world GDP.[3]

The huge concentrations of capital that globalised financial markets made possible are not neutral quantities. In 1999, for example, a small number of highly secretive US-based 'hedge funds' – firms speculating in foreign exchange derivatives – had

---

*   Strictly speaking there was actually a three and a half hour gap between the close of the stock exchange in New York and the opening of the exchange in Tokyo, and another hour-long gap between closing in Tokyo and re-opening in London.

between them access to something like $30 trillion of bank loans to bet against national currencies. Peter Gowan reasons convincingly that their successive attacks on foreign currencies must have had the tacit approval of the US government; in effect they were semi-official financial pirates, a modern version of the 'privateers' licensed by the British government in the eighteenth century to raid enemy merchant shipping.[4] The scale of the funds they could borrow explains why the notorious collapse in 1998 of the Long Term Capital Management fund, with its Nobel laureate directors, necessitated the mobilisation of $3.5 billions by the US government to bail out banks that would otherwise have collapsed.

Non-financial trans-national corporations

By the end of the 1980s trans-national corporations, or TNCs, were responsible for more than half of all the world's trade in manufactures, and perhaps three quarters of all trade in services: according to one estimate, in 1994 the 500 largest TNCs controlled three-quarters of all world trade. TNCs also controlled 80 percent of all land under export crops, and the marketing channels for a large number of primary commodities.[5] Foreign direct investment (FDI) by TNCs also made them omnipresent; by the mid-1980s the value of production by TNCs' foreign affiliates had overtaken the value of world exports. At the same moment FDI in service industries overtook FDI in manufacturing, and for the first time FDI as a whole expanded faster than financial flows.[6]

A high proportion of the assets of both the manufacturing and the service sectors in most OECD countries thus came to be owned by big transnational companies. By the late 1990s about a third of all international trade consisted of intra-firm transactions (and of course more in the case of major industrial exporters - over 50 percent of the trade of the USA and Japan).[7] Large TNCs are, moreover, by definition oligopolists, with considerable market power. The most significant indicators of concentration have become world market shares rather than national ones, and 'in a wide range of industries and product groups the world market is shared by 10-12 firms, and often fewer.'[8]

Yet such data still tend to understate the scale of TNC dominance of the global economy, because they do not take into account the growth of corporate networks. A firm may derive substantial profits from a country without owning any plant or employing a single worker in it, through franchising, licensing and similar contractual relationships.[9] 'Network' firms, consisting of webs of legally independent units linked by cross-ownership or contracts, have become increasingly common, as have alliances of a looser kind between companies on the lines of the Japanese keiretsu, relying on long-standing trading relations and trust, without cross-ownership or overall contractual links.[10] A statement like the following (in the *Economist*), that 'the world's top 300 industrial corporations now control... 25 percent of the world's $20 trillion stock of productive assets' has therefore become hard to interpret.[11] Their power to determine the use of the world's productive assets may well be larger. The UN estimated in 1994 that 'overall, as much as one-third of world output may now be under the direct governance of TNCs, with the indirect influence certainly much greater',[12] and since then the scale of foreign direct investment has continued to increase.*

---

* These UN figures naturally do not cover transnational criminal organizations, although some of these function in many respects like legal TNCs and have comparable assets. Louise Shelley notes that the Medellin syndicate, the less successful of the two Colombian drug cartels, was said to have at least $10 billion worth of assets in Europe, Asia and North America in the late 1980s, equal to the average assets of the four Swedish TNCs included in the UN's top 100 list in 1992 (See Louise I. Shelley, 'Transnational Organized Crime: An Imminent Threat to the Nation-State?', *Journal of International Affairs* 48/2, 1995, pp. 480-81). Barnet and Cavanagh report estimates of between $100 and $300 billion as the annual world-wide profits from the drugs trade, implying the existence of numerous powerful transnational enterprises (Barnet and Cavanagh, *Global Dreams*, p. 389). The growing significance of organised crime in the global economy, and the parallels between it and both TNCs and states, were noted by Susan Strange in 'The Limits of Politics', in *Government and Opposition* 30/3, 1995, pp. 305-07.

The need to operate globally in order to survive also meant that the number of TNCs expanded dramatically, from 7,000 in 1970 to 60,000 by the late 1990s, with 508,000 affiliates;[13] and this in turn means that even a quite small company by world standards may be fulfilling specific tasks in a tightly-integrated global production and marketing strategy directed from overseas (for example Volvo, now owned by Ford). The most important directing centres are the headquarters of a limited number of very large TNCs; in 1990 fewer than 300 American firms accounted for three-quarters of all transnational activity by US companies, and about 150 British firms accounted for four-fifths of all British FDI.[14] In 1997 Britain was 'host' to the parent firms of ten of the world's 100 largest multinationals, and host to over a thousand TNCs in all. Conversely 2,525 affiliates of foreign-based TNCs operated in Britain; of the major OECD countries, Britain in 1997 was far the most 'transnational' (i.e. it had much the largest proportion of its GDP produced by foreign TNC affiliates, the largest foreign TNC share of gross fixed capital investment, and so on).[15]

The significance of TNCs in national politics can be summed up in two broad generalisations. First, they are often very large organisations – in 1997 the largest 100 TNCs world-wide had total sales of $39 billion and assets of $42 billion – and so they often have larger negotiating resources than states, as well as having considerable economic leverage, regularly borrowing and spending more than the states of quite large countries. In January 2000, for example, America Online raised $160 billion – a third as much as the entire GDP of India, and twice that of Chile – to take over Time Warner. Of course the economies of countries like India or Britain are far larger than the gross revenues of even the largest TNC, but TNCs are free to deploy their resources single-mindedly in pursuit of their limited goals in a way no government can. In Britain, an officer who had been assigned by the Office of Fair Trading to report on predatory pricing by the big supermarket chains admitted that 'including myself, there will be only four of us working on this and that's along with the other cases we look at. We have to do this on a shoestring while the companies we look into have a hundred times more resources than we have.'[16] In the year 1990 US banks – which were by then heavily represented in London – spent $15 billion on information technology; as late as 1996 the entire British government's total annual expenditure on information technology was estimated at about $3 billion.[17] In general, states have long since lost whatever communications advantage they may once have had over big corporations.

Corporations are also sophisticated lobbyists at the supranational as well as national levels of power, often with diplomatic backing by their 'home' states.[18] The chief executive of a major TNC seldom has to wait long for an appointment with a senior official of the World Bank or the European Commission, or a minister of a national state; Monbiot's painfully revealing study of the corporate penetration of the British state is full of examples.* In short, Susan Strange was right to insist, already in the early 1990s, that '...transnational corporations should now be put centre stage' in any realistic analysis of domestic politics, not just in the analysis of international relations.[19]

The second politically significant feature of TNCs is that they are profitable in large part precisely because of their political capacity, especially in their negotiations with host or prospective host governments, to get regulations altered (or maintained) to their advantage, as well as subsidies and tax holidays. SmithKline Beecham, the world's tenth largest pharmaceutical company, spent thirty millon ecus on a successful campaign to get the European Parliament to allow the commercial patenting of genes.[20] Alternatively they can exploit the existing pattern of regulatory differences between countries, getting labour-intensive work done

---

* For instance among many other achievements the food giant Monsanto, whose representatives met ministers and officials from the departments of Agriculture and the Environment on twenty-two occasions in the twenty months following the 1997 election, succeeded in preventing the introduction of regulations requiring GM food to be labelled as such. See George Monbiot, *Captive State: The Corporate Takeover of Britain* (Macmillan, 2000), passim.

where unions are weak and wages low, declaring taxable profits where taxes are lowest through 'transfer pricing', and so on.

The phenomenon of 'network' firms – consisting of many legally separate companies, but with complex interlocking shareholdings allowing for unified overall control – is to a significant extent about reducing regulatory costs. It is usually justified in terms of the 'positive externalities' this can yield from specialisation, greater flexibility, and so on; but 'dissolving' itself into a network can also allow a TNC to escape taxes and other costs. 'Because the firm determines its own size [in deciding what bit of a network, legally speaking, it will 'be'], it also chooses the limits of its legal responsibilities, which in turn provides an open invitation for the evasion of mandatory legal duties'.[21]

Liability to taxes is especially significant, since the power to tax is the foundation of national sovereignty; yet the complexity of contemporary TNC financing, combined with the network form of organisation, enables them to limit the bite of all but the biggest and most determined national tax authorities. Sol Picciotto notes that 'the growth of the TNC, in the characteristic form of an international network of related companies carrying on businesses in different countries in a more or less integrated way, is to a significant extent attributable to the opportunities it has to take advantage of regulatory differences, or 'regulatory arbitrage'.[22] As a result of this, and the greatly increased lobbying power of capital, both corporate tax rates and marginal personal tax rates for high-income investors fell in almost every OECD country from the mid-1980s to the mid-1990s;[23] and 'perhaps half of the industrialized world's stock of money resides in or passes through tax havens'.[24] It is sobering to reflect how far the devastating impact on public spending of voters' 'tax aversion', and the weakening of social solidarity that has resulted, were due to the fact that so much corporate income was now escaping tax altogether.

In short, we have to recognise how far the balance of power between governments and corporations has shifted. Perhaps the best

comparison is between most states today and municipalities in the past. In the era of national economies, corporate investment decisions were made on the basis of variations between different locations in a given country in terms of labour supplies, infrastructures, proximity to markets, local taxes and the like. Today, in the global economy, national 'regulatory regimes' themselves have become part of the pattern of local conditions (or 'complications', as Hobsbawm says) which trans-national corporations take into account, and are constantly working to change.

Global market forces and national policy-making

The ways in which financial and non-financial market forces affect national policy-making are somewhat different.

Financial markets are supposed to register the collective judgment of the owners of capital on the profitability of the overall mix of economic and political conditions of any country when all factors, including the risk of adverse government policies, are taken into account, and these markets are now increasingly globalised: 'With instantaneous communication and information flows among all the major markets, passive capital and unexploited investment opportunities will not long be kept apart by national borders... If there is a viable futures or options market to be made, it is of little relevance where it is made.'[25] Global markets are thus supposed to ensure that holders of financial assets receive roughly the same risk-adjusted real return everywhere, so any country that offers significantly lower returns is likely to experience capital outflow and a depreciating exchange rate, with a consequent economic downturn. This means that Keynesian macroeconomic policies are no longer an option, at least not for the government of any one country acting alone. Devaluation is taboo, and so are budget deficits: 'the power of the bond market has forced discipline on to governments everywhere.'[26] Philip Cerny summed up the consensus as follows:

Governments have all found their capacity to intervene in the domestic economy significantly altered, reducing their power to pursue comprehensive economic strategies and differentiating and complicating the kind of market interventions which they are led or forced to adopt. The interaction of changing financial market structures on the one hand and states on the other has done more than production, trade or international cooperative regimes to undermine the structures of the Keynesian welfare state and to impose the norms of the competition state...[27]

But this loss of 'Keynesian capacity', important though it is, has tended to divert attention from the tendency of financial markets to constrain all areas of policy, not just macroeconomic policy; and this they do continually, with the help of the grades awarded to governments and public organisations by the credit rating agencies. Plans which the experts employed by these agencies dislike, whether or not they affect public spending, have an automatic negative effect on interest rates.[28] Nothing is excluded from consideration. Their surveillance of social and political change, as well economic indicators and policies, becomes more and more comprehensive, and whether or not it gives rational signals or leads to rational responses by investors, governments increasingly feel its constraining influence. Even matters that might once have seemed purely the province of politics, such as professional training and qualifications, or the protection of the national language, can turn out to be of concern to 'the market', not to mention matters as vital to investors as, for example, proposals to tighten the regulation of money markets or to impose new obligations on the managers of pension funds.[29]

More generally, market analysts routinely estimate a 'political risk factor' for every country, expressed as a premium on the current interest rate on government bonds, which discounts the possibility of future political changes unfavourable to capital. Any proposal to increase taxation, especially on capital, or any proposal that could increase the budget deficit, necessitating increased public borrowing, will tend to result in increased interest rates. 'Left-

labour' governments in the 'north' have consistently had to face a risk premium of one or two per cent.[30] Before the 1992 election in Britain the opposition Labour leader John Smith is said to have arranged that in the event of a Labour victory the Treasury would immediately increase the interest rate by two per cent, to avert capital flight; and in 1996-97 the pre-election policy commitments made by Gordon Brown, as Labour's shadow Chancellor of the Exchequer, were heavily (and successfully) directed to avoiding a large interest rate penalty being imposed by the financial markets if Labour won.

Non-financial capital differs from financial capital in being committed to particular lines of production of goods or services, and over the relatively long term. The pressures it brings to bear on national governments can be examined in relation to, first, non-tariff barriers to trade, and second, non-tariff barriers to investment.

As tariff barriers to global trade grew steadily lower under the Bretton Woods arrangements, non-tariff barriers of various kinds came more clearly into view, affecting an estimated 18 per cent of world trade in 1992.[31] Some of them, such as state purchasing rules that confine bids for government contracts to domestic companies, may serve legitimate national interests in defence, food security, and so on; others, like complex bureaucratic customs procedures, or safety or health tests not applied to domestically-produced goods, are essentially protectionist measures. A third category consists of domestic social practices or arrangements, sometimes reinforced by law, that express long-standing and cherished national values – sensitive issues of national culture and social practice, from national conceptions of safety or hygiene or environmental conservation to the national language, culture (films and magazines) and tastes. Such embedded social practices were famously defined by the Americans, in their efforts to open up Japanese markets to US exports, as 'structural impediments' [to free trade].*

---

* American companies could not get orders from the Japanese keiretsu (or corporate groups) which did business with each other based primarily on long-term

The main pressure to lift non-tariff barriers to trade comes from foreign companies anxious to break into local markets. Governments also get involved, through lobbying and diplomatic efforts, in trying to reduce other states' non-tariff barriers and defend their own. The member states of the EU initially aimed at eliminating such barriers through 'harmonisation' – i.e. adopting common standards and rules; but this proved too difficult and was dropped in favour of 'mutual recognition' – i.e., subject to certain grounds of exception, any product or service that could legally be sold in one country could be sold in them all. 'Mutual recognition' legitimated the least onerous regulations and gave all EU states an incentive to adopt them.

But major non-financial TNCs are concerned less with access for their exports than with productive investment in 'host' countries, which makes them interested in a much wider range of policy issues than the regulations specifically applying to their products. John Dunning, a leading expert on TNCs, summarised their outlook as follows:

> ... if the government of one country imposes too high a corporation tax, firms - be they domestic or foreign - may decide to relocate their value-added activities in another county where taxes are lower; or, in considering where to site their new plants, firms may choose that country with the least burdensome environmental constraints, or whose government pursues the most favourable industrial policy, or which offers the most advanced telecommunications facilities or the most attractive tax breaks for R and D activities. Indeed... anything and everything a government does which affects the competitiveness of those firms which must have some latitude in their cross-border locational choices must come under scrutiny.[32]

---

relationships of trust, and only secondarily on price. Japan's Large Retail Store Law – which protects small Japanese retailers from elimination by supermarket chains in order to maintain employment in the retail sector and preserve a pedestrian-based local shopping culture – was also targeted, because of the desire of US retailers like Toys-R-Us to open branches in Japan. On the other hand when in 2006 a Dubai-based firm bought the British firm P&O, which had operations in six major US ports, the Congress abandoned free trade principles and P&O was forced to surrender this part of its portfolio to be picked up by US-based buyers.

The scope of the 'regulatory regimes' which states compete to 'lighten' for non-financial TNCs may, then, like the scope of the financial markets' concerns, be very wide. And as we have already seen, states may often be 'outgunned' by the legal and technical expertise that TNCs can command.*

Yet the tendency of 'regulatory competition' to cause a 'dive to the bottom' is offset by political pressures on states to prevent the lowering of standards, whether to protect some special interest or one more widely shared. Even under the favourable influence of the EU's Single Market Act, which obliges states to recognise each others' standards, effective resistance is mounted, by lobbying and legal proceedings, and outcomes are determined by complex combinations of reason, interest, the relative strengths of the participants, etc., and do not always lead to lower standards.[33]

Nonetheless it is clear that states no longer have the last word; indeed there is no last word, since there is always a potentially lower standard than the prevailing one which some country may choose to adopt. Corporations constantly return to the attack on standards they want to lower, eventually wearing out the usually poorly-resourced and largely amateur opposition mounted by public groups. The Mutilateral Agreement on Investment, which would have given global corporations far-reaching legal rights against signatory governments, was defeated, but the US then made numerous bilateral agreements with many individual states which had the same effect. The initial version of the EU's Bolkestein Directive, which aimed to treat most if not all public services within the EU as trade matters, and hence required them to be opened

---

*   Yves Dezelay has pointed out that the huge global firms of corporate lawyers that have also emerged since the 1980s do not just supply a demand created by regulatory arbitrage, and by regulatory competition between states; they also play an important role in driving the whole process: 'One of the main factors disrupting the national systems of regulation results from the competitive pressure exerted by the forum-shopping for regulatory regimes to which multinationals of expert services incite their clients'. ('Professional Competition and the Social Construction of Transnational Regulatory Expertise', in Joseph McCahery, Sol Picciotto and Colin Scott (eds.), *Corporate Control and Accountability* [Clarendon Press, 1993], p. 203).

to market forces, was also blocked, but is being reintroduced with some services partially (and questionably) excluded.

To sum up this discussion: the power of 'market forces', whether affecting macro-economic policy generally through the financial markets, or micro-economic policy through pressure from global corporations and their home governments, has greatly increased, and the autonomy of most states – except, perhaps, the USA, or oil-rich states like Saudi Arabia – has greatly declined.* Trans-national corporations – financial and non-financial – have become central political forces. On the fundamental issues of economic life – which as we have seen reach deeply into the texture of social policy too – national governments have become more continually and more decisively responsive to corporations than to voters. This has always been true in most of the 'South'. Now it is true everywhere. No portrait of modern politics – or the modern state – is realistic that does not start from this premise.

Two complementary dynamics were set in motion by the shift in the balance of power from national electorates to global capital. On the one hand, the greatly increased power of global market forces more or less rapidly reshapes the social relations of production in all countries – the structure of production, the class structure, the hegemonic ideology, the shape of 'civil society'. On the other hand government policy, responding to global market forces, progressively reshapes the national state in conformity with the demands of corporate power – 'downsizing' the state, converting the public sector into a field of capital accumulation, and reducing government accountability to the electorate. The first process facilitates the second. The state is radically reshaped,

---

* There are obviously big differences between states, in terms of the scale of their internal market, the extent of their economies' exposure to global market forces, their possession of strategic resources, etc., which affect their capacity to resist external pressures. I would argue that these pressures always operate at the margin and affect even the most powerful states over time, but what is said here about states in general is meant to refer to states with medium-sized industrial economies and no unique economic or political leverage vis à vis TNCs or other states.

and the boundary between it and the private interests of capital is fatally eroded. This is the subject of last two sections of this essay, and is pursued further in the essay which concludes this volume. But first we need to be realistically aware of the fast-changing social context.

The social and political impact

Global competition leads to a world-wide process of concentration, through mergers and acquisitions on an unprecedented scale, as corporations jockey for position to become world-wide oligopolists. In countries of the 'North' productivity gains are achieved, with magnified social costs, as companies shed all sentimentality in face of intensified cross-border competition. Abrupt announcements of thousands of 'job losses' become commonplace as manufacturers shift production to lower-cost sites, and retail chains and banks and other service industries seek profits from merging overheads, closing branches and transferring costs to customers. 'Factor-price equalisation' (a.k.a. the law of value), now operating on a global scale, drives wages towards world rather than national norms, and gradually restructures the workforces of even the richest countries in line with the new geographical options open to capital. The result in the main industrialised countries has been a marked shift in the division of national income between capital and labour, and for less-skilled workers a decline in real wages, casualisation and higher unemployment. At the same time world demand for highly skilled labour has raised its price, while the increased returns to capital, and the reduction of taxes on them, have dramatically expanded the global cadre of millionaires (to nearly nine million in 2006) and billionaires (793 in the same year).[34] The combination of these processes has produced patterns of inequality (and disparities of power) not seen since the 1930s in some countries of the 'north' (signalled by new terms, such as 'the socially excluded', 'winners and losers', 'A and B teams', 'the two-thirds/one-third society', and the like);[35] new levels of crime and preoccupation with crime;

new patterns of regional differentiation within countries as well as between them; and new problems of, and preoccupation with, migration. Even a century that had become accustomed to change was aware at its close of a fresh unleashing of the forces famously described a century and a half earlier:

> Constant revolutionising of production, uninterrupted disturbance of all social conditions, everlasting uncertainty and agitation... All old-established national industries have been destroyed or are daily being destroyed. They are dislodged by new industries, whose introduction becomes a life and death question for all civilized nations...[36]

The rest of this section traces these effects in the case of Britain.

There, the most immediately obvious effect of the restructuring of global production was the further decline of manufacturing, from 25 per cent of the GDP in 1980 to 16 per cent in 2003.[37] Whole industries for which Britain had been famous, from coal-mining (which at the beginning of the twentieth century had employed a million people) to the manufacture of motorcycles, had disappeared, while labour-saving technology in other sectors had led to a continued decline in old-style manual work (down from about 50 per cent of all jobs in 1979 to 36 per cent in 1991),[38] as well as facilitating the continued 'feminisation' of waged work – raising the proportion of women in the workforce from 37 per cent in 1981 to almost 50 per cent by 2005. The shift to services meant, too, that by 2000 fewer than one worker in ten worked in a factory. Competitive pressures and the 'flexibilisation' of labour also meant that 'putting out' returned with a vengeance – in 2005 three million people were 'homeworkers' – and casualisation became relatively common again, half a century after it had been virtually eliminated. All these factors, above all the contraction of manufacturing and the curtailment of trade union rights, combined to produce a dramatic drop in union membership; by the end of the 1990s less than a third of all employees were in unions, a drop of 21 per cent in ten years. Industrial action declined to very low levels and resistance to privatisation, job losses and casualisation became generally spasmodic and weak.

As regards incomes, the chief effects of globalisation were first, a big increase in total real household disposable income (an increase of 52 per cent over the years 1980 to 2000); but, second, its much more unequal distribution. In 1971 the richest ten per cent of the population had incomes on average three times bigger than those of the poorest ten per cent. By 2003-04 their incomes were four times bigger and there was considerable poverty: 17 per cent of the population were living on 'low' incomes, defined as less than 60 per cent of the median income.

Wealth was even more unequally distributed. Share ownership spread to 17 per cent of all adults, i.e. well beyond the ranks of the 'upper middle class', which had significant effects on people's attitudes to shareholding, even if most of these shareholdings were on a very modest scale.[39] But in 2003-04 the richest one per cent of the population owned 23 per cent of all marketable wealth, and the richest fifty percent owned 94 per cent of it. At the other end of the scale a quarter of the population – including the long-term unemployed, pensioners dependent on state pensions and the great majority of single mothers and their children – lived increasingly different lives from those of the top fifty or sixty per cent; one child in three was growing up in poverty. Yet poverty was now seen as a 'minority' issue, rather than a shared problem of the working class majority whom the labour movement and the Labour Party had represented in the past. The task of speaking for the poor was taken over by 'single issue' groups – Shelter, the Child Poverty Action Group, Mind, Age Concern, etc. – which both the media and the government called 'special interests groups', and largely disregarded. The putative social solidarity once symbolised by universal flat-rate National Insurance contributions had largely disappeared.

Yet it was a fact that most people's real incomes had risen, and rather sharply. In 1998-99 spending on leisure goods and services was for the first time the single largest item of average household expenditure (just ahead of food, housing, and housing goods and services). Supermarkets had displaced butchers, bakers, grocers and greengrocers, and were beginning to compete in selling leisure goods and domestic hardware; 86 per cent of all consumer spending was with major chains. Shopping malls proliferated. Over half the population took part in the national lottery, spending an average of £200 a year on it. Holidays abroad had become normal. British seaside resorts rotted.[40] Personal consumption had become a way of life. And since more and more people could, for example, now afford to buy school books for their children, pay for their own dentistry, or buy individual health insurance, the idea that they should have to do so – because state schools and dental services and hospital care were increasingly under-funded – no longer seemed shocking or even surprising. Nor did media coverage of the conspicuous consumption of the super-rich (restaurant bills of £2000, the ownership of multiple houses worth millions of pounds and sports cars worth several tens of thousands) or the wretched state of homeless people any longer raise many eyebrows, let alone stir much indignation. Television documentaries on social problems ceased to attract viewers. One leading documentary film-maker remarked, 'Programmes were made about people sleeping in the streets of London at a time when hardly anybody did. And now thousands sleep on the streets and no one makes any programmes about them.'[41]

The connotations of class inevitably changed too. Being 'working class' probably meant that your income was paid weekly rather than monthly and that you were not eligible for various privileges reserved for management, such as private health insurance or holidays longer than the legal minimum – unless you happened to belong to a union that had won such concessions. Especially in old industrial areas where the manual working class used to be concentrated there was still a recognisably distinct working class culture, even though diluted by globally-driven tastes in music, dress, food and travel. But being 'working class' no longer necessarily meant – as it once had, rather reliably – being a manual worker, living in rented housing, or being a member of a trade union – or even voting for the Labour Party. By April 2000 polls showed that Labour support among manual workers was barely higher than among managerial and professional workers, and only moderately higher than among 'intermediate and routine non-manual' (lower management and office staff) workers. Even working-class voters had 'become more and more like discriminating consumers who evaluate competing products.'[42]

The implications for social-democratic politics were profound. The perceived class interests of voters had once set limits to what business could expect either party to do in office. But the class foundations of the major parties no longer offered such firm barriers. In every sphere, from town planning and food safety to university research and schools, a 'corporate takeover' of policy occurred which would have been unthinkable while those barriers remained.[43]

Most people worked for private companies, and what remained of the public sector had been remodelled on 'business' lines, with 'profit centres', performance-related pay, annual 'market-testing', 'outsourcing', 'downsizing' and 'productivity savings' targets – and in sectors like hospitals, appeals to charities for donations. And following the privatisation of the formerly nationalised utilities people now bought their phone services, water, gas and electricity from private companies. Buses, trains and train stations, airlines and airports were also now all privately owned and operated. Prisoners were detained in private prisons. Fees now had to be paid for many public services which used to be largely free – dentistry, eye care, university education, the use of government statistics, research libraries, access to government statistics, musical instrument teaching in schools. Official terminology was changed to encourage the shift from a 'producer' to a 'consumer' culture: 'customer' replaced 'passenger', 'client' replaced 'patient'. People took the hint and (encouraged by lawyers) began suing the state;

litigation against doctors, hospitals and the police, especially, increased dramatically.*

Cuts in public spending opened the way to other kinds of commercial penetration of the 'life world'. Most major sporting events had already become corporate ideological property (e.g. the 'Bank of Scotland Premier [football] League', the 'PPP Healthcare County [cricket] Championships'); the same was increasingly true of television shows, art exhibitions, conferences, concerts and operas. By the late 1990s sponsorship had spread to schools and universities, train stations, the Labour Party's annual conference, the National Health Service and even police cars.** Scientific research depended more and more on corporate funding, while public funding for large-scale social and economic research was increasingly oriented towards the search for 'economic competitiveness'.[44] In London's docklands, the site of a vast private development boom in the late 1980s, investors even speculated in housing 'futures'.***

---

* Data on litigation against the police are not centrally collected but large payments are regularly reported in the press. The National Audit office found that in 1998-99 NHS trusts paid out £1 billion in legal claims – equivalent to about 2 percent of the total NHS budget - while in 1999 the Medical Defence Union paid out £77 million in cases against individual doctors, almost double the figure for 1996.

** Police cars in Kensington in central London were sponsored by Harrods, the country's most famous department store, even though successive Home Secretaries, supported by the courts, had deemed Harrods' owner, Mr El Fayeed, unsuitable to be granted British citizenship. In 1998 delegates to the Labour Party's annual conference found their name tags advertising Somerfield, a supermarket chain; the 1998 conference to celebrate 50 years of the National Health Service was 'sponsored' by the private medical insurance industry and the pharmaceutical industry; in 2000 the Lake District National Park Commission was reported to be considering inviting corporate sponsorship for the Park's best known lakes and mountains. Other examples are cited by Monbiot in his *Captive State*, pp. 1-4. It is interesting to speculate why the British were willing to go so far in such directions. In some cases government agencies, faced with annual cuts in their budgets that no 'productivity' increases could offset, turned to sponsorship and other forms of private sector links out of financial desperation; but the generally uncritical acceptance of sponsorship was nonetheless remarkable.

*** Whimster perceptively noted this as an example of the new individualised culture in its most alienated form: 'Career now has to be thought of as an asset, as a flow of future income, to be offset against the burdens of housing, private schooling

There was little serious resistance to all these changes. Within two decades the omnipresence of business and business culture had become as commonplace and apparently inevitable as the rain.

The decline in class-based politics, and its replacement by politics conceived on the model of a department store, in which the parties conceive of themselves as offering voters a wide range of 'products', meant a corresponding rise in the importance of political advertising through the mass media, and especially television. By the early 1980s British people spent, on average, nearly three and a half hours of every day watching television, and a further hour listening to radio. Most of what people watched was entertainment, and the 'production values' of sports and film gradually displaced those of reporting and argument. Celebrity – of film, music and sports stars, and television presenters – became very important. Party leaders seek photo-opportunities with stars, or even purport to take them on as policy advisers (for example Tony Blair presented the pop-star Bono as his leading adviser on poverty relief), in effect getting them to endorse their political product. Politicians do their best to try to become celebrities themselves, changing their appearance and way of speaking; being 'telegenic' becomes a prime qualification for leadership.

Neither parties nor trade unions any longer function as mass educators or seek to organise people's ideas and attitudes on a wide range of issues through continuous interaction with their memberships – a role largely abandoned to the mass-circulation newspapers with their often ultramontane right-wing bias. Two-thirds of teenagers have little or no interest in politics and scant

---

and consumerism. Children, parents, education, housing and residential location in relation to collective services all enter into [the] uneasy calculation ... Trading in the future contracts of homes, as occurred in Docklands, is to treat one's life-world as a commodity' (Sam Whimster, 'Yuppies: A Keyword of the 1980s', in Leslie Budd and Sam Whimster (eds.), *Global Finance and Urban Living: A Study of Metropolitan Change*, London: Routledge, 1992, p. 329).

political knowledge.[45] One voter in five is functionally illiterate.* Images, music and other non-verbal signifiers increasingly displace words. Party political TV broadcasts have ceased to be reasoned appeals to either principle or pragmatism but become increasingly like commercials. The disjunction between policy-making – hopefully at least, based on analytic reasoning and facts – and the way voters were appealed to has become more marked than at any time since the introduction of universal suffrage.

Media and public relations skills have become much more highly valued and influential. Not just parties, but also central and local government departments, trade unions, universities, hospitals, churches and prisons, all model themselves on large companies and employ 'directors of communications' or 'public affairs', and 'press officers' or 'media liaison officers', who make corporate videos, maintain web-sites, 'strategise' over the production of 'logos', provide briefings, distribute 'information kits', give press conferences and photo-opportunities, seek radio and television interviews, sponsor conferences, monitor news stories, keep data bases and engage in 'instant rebuttals.'[46] 'Spin' has become an object of universal resentment and scorn, but there is no avoiding it because what appears on the screen or in the press is what matters. Policy announcements are 'trailed' days or even weeks in advance ('the Prime Minister will announce that...') so that by the time they are officially made, adverse reactions have been anticipated and helpful glosses added. Public meetings, in the sense of open access meetings between politicians and the public, with opportunities for questions and heckling – an old-fashioned test of competence and the common touch – have given way to carefully-managed television appearances with handpicked interlocutors and carefully selected audiences.

---

* In 1997 one in five British adults could not locate the page for plumbers in the Yellow Pages phone book or calculate change; one in sixteen could not read a simple notice. One adult in three could not calculate the area of a room 21feet by 14, even using a calculator. See *A Fresh Start: Improving Literacy and Numeracy for Adults* (Department for Education and Employment, 1999), pp. 1- 4.

Reshaping the state

A further dynamic set in motion by globalisation comes from the response of national governments to the agenda set by newly ascendant global capital. This agenda was known for some time as 'the Washington consensus'. The consensus was that not only should trade barriers be removed, but national states should also be restructured to serve capital by privatising publicly-owned enterprises, giving constitutional rights to foreign corporations, opening public services to private provision, downsizing the state apparatus and 'outsourcing' its activities to private firms, cutting taxes and reducing state-provided social security.

Britain moved farther and faster along this path than any other major country. The Thatcher governments of 1979-90 pushed through institutional and constitutional changes that were arguably more far-reaching and radical than any since the Tudors; and what the Conservatives began, Labour continued.

By 2000 nearly all the country's infrastructural and service operations had been sold to private companies, from energy and the telephone system to the railways. The Conservatives also revolutionised the fiscal system, redistributing the tax burden from capital to wages and salaries, and from high incomes to low, and cutting back most forms of social security. In office after 1997 Labour continued with the privatisation of state-owned assets and state services and also pushed strongly ahead with the Private Finance Initiative, which channelled tax revenues into private hands by inviting the private sector to build hospitals and schools and offices and lease them back to the state, complete with privately-employed support staff. It also sought to reorient the social security system, reducing the allowances for single parents and disabled people and adopting a 'welfare to work' approach to youth unemployment.[47] It introduced private companies into the management of state schools and colleges and into the provision of state-funded health care, breaking up the National Health Service into a fragmented market system.

CIVIL SERVICE

The Conservatives took away the most significant powers of elected local government (the provision of rented housing and the management of schools), and effectively ended local councils' freedom to raise local taxes and set their own budgets. After 1997 New Labour made no attempt to restore local democracy; on the contrary, it abolished the right of the public and press to attend all council meetings and legislated to replace decision-making by committees of elected councillors with small executive teams – reflecting the same philosophy that had guided the reconstruction of the party.[48]

The Conservatives set in hand a radical reform of the civil service. In 1975 the civil service was still a coherent legal-rational hierarchy led by a small corps of patrician public servants dedicated to prudent socio-economic management and gradual adaptation of policy to evolutionary social change. By 2000 it had been broken up into a set of small, central, policy-making ministries, led by a small elite of civil servants promoted for their entrepreneurial style; and a huge range of unelected national and local executive agencies, whether hived off from government ministries, like the Prisons Service, or newly-created 'quasi-non-governmental bodies' ('quangos'), such as the Office for Standards in Education; all organised on business lines with chief executives on short-term contracts and frequently operating as 'profit centres' which charge other branches of the state for their services. They also imposed an internal 'quasi-market' system on the National Health Service and the organisation of personal social services in local government, and ensured that the nominally independent BBC followed suit. These policies too were retained in essentials by Labour after 1997. By the early 1990s 'quangos' were responsible for a third of all public spending, almost as much as elected local government.[49] In opposition before 1997 Labour had promised to 'roll back the quango state'; but once in office they not only left the new system essentially alone, but soon set about enthusiastically extending it.*

A counterpart to the quasi-commercialisation of central and local government was the proliferation of auditing, i.e. the use of business-derived concepts of independent supervision to measure and evaluate performance by public agencies and public employees, from civil servants and school teachers to university lecturers and doctors: 'environmental audit, value for money audit, management audit, forensic audit, data audit, intellectual property audit, medical audit, teaching audit and technology audit emerged and, to varying degrees, acquired a degree of institutional stability and acceptance... very few people have been left untouched by these developments...'[50] In place of a society of citizens with the democratic power to ensure the effective and proper use of collective resources, and relying on a large measure of trust in the public sector, there emerged a society of 'auditees', anxiously preparing for audits and inspections.** 'League tables' (by analogy with professional football) were developed, purporting to show the relative efficiency or inefficiency of universities or schools or hospitals, or even individual surgeons, based on quantitative measures of performance of often dubious validity; and a culture of competition, rewards and punishments developed around them, avidly publicised by the right-wing media. Inspection agencies were charged with 'naming and shaming' 'failing'

---

* Quango appointments were now advertised and made by an independent commission, but the appointments process itself remained secret and unaccountable. 'Dissidents' were not encouraged.

** 'Auditing is a process of operationalising the accountability of an agent to a principal where the principal can't do it alone and where trust is lacking... Much of the audit explosion presumes that teachers, social workers, etc. can't be trusted – with often, or sometimes, perverse effects.... audits [can] create the distrust they presuppose and ... this in turn leads to various organisational pathologies... Where the solution to these pathologies of distrust is yet more and better auditing, yet more guardians of impersonal trust, then one has the audit society in a nutshell' (Michael Power, *Audit Society*, pp. 135-36).

individual teachers, schools, social work departments, etc. Private firms were invited to take over and run 'failing' institutions.*

Labour in office not only retained this approach but extended it. In 1975 the trade unions still enjoyed the broad legal immunities originally established in the Trade Disputes Act of 1906. By 2000 these were history, replaced by what Tony Blair approvingly called 'the most restrictive trade union laws in the western world'.[51] In 1975 civil liberties were among the most liberal in the world and the police were still subject to a degree of accountability to elected local authorities. By 2000 a series of Acts – the Public Order Act 1986, the Criminal Justice Act 1994, the Security Service Act 1996, the Police Act 1997 and the Terrorism Act 2000 (all passed *before* September 11, 2001) – had considerably narrowed the scope for peaceful dissent and strengthened the powers of the police, who had also been made significantly more answerable to central government.

In short, the Conservatives undertook a massive shrinking, centralisation and *de-democratisation* of the state, which Labour pushed even further, in spite of previous promises to reverse

---

* Why these divisive and largely counter-productive ideas and practices should have been adopted with such enthusiasm is a puzzle, and not just to foreigners. It began, of course, with the Thatcherites' deep hostility to the public sector – which they saw, correctly, as a bastion of social-democratic ideas - and their almost religious belief in the values of small business. They did not like public servants of the traditional type and therefore would not trust them; in the absence of trust, they must be subjected to business-style auditing. Labour's modernisers had more mixed feelings, perhaps, but especially in the first two years after 1997, while public spending was held down to impress the financial markets, they wanted more output for fewer resources; and since relatively few teachers, social workers, etc., were 'New Labour' enthusiasts, continuing the audit and penalty system may well have seemed the only way to get it. As Radice has pointed out in relation to higher education, however, it has produced a peculiarly British version of the Soviet mode of production, including rigid hierarchies, one-man management, quantitative targets, the concealment of resources, bullying, nepotism, cynicism, stress and demoralisation. (Hugo Radice, 'From Warwick University Ltd. to British Universities plc', Institute for Politics and International Studies, Leeds University 2000). The peculiar officiousness needed by the bureaucracy of appraisers and evaluators to whom the 'audit' industry gives power are surely present in any culture, but it is sometimes hard not to feel they are more than normally abundant in Britain.

it.* In most respects Labour and the Conservatives converged in reshaping of the framework of British politics on the basis of principles – centralisation and executive control – which reflected the circumstances in which politics now had to be conducted – the 'new reality' of the globalised economy. The divisions that had rent Labour in the 1970s and 1980s and the Conservatives in the 1990s were effects of the impact of global market forces on British society. Rising inequality and the contraction of the welfare state which neoliberalism entailed split the Labour Party between democratic socialists and right-wing social democrats who were ready to come to terms with the power of global capital, while big business's interest in closer relations with the European Union split the Conservatives. What all party leaders and prime ministers now needed was freedom to temper policy to the requirements of markets – over which they had less and less control – on the one hand, and the wishes of the electorate on the other.

Party politics
Political parties mirror the society in which they operate even more, perhaps, than the state; so it should be no surprise that parties, which played such a central role in the formation of the global economy,

---

* The only important exception was Labour's creation of a Scottish Parliament and a Welsh Assembly with devolved powers of self-government, but devolution was the exception that proved the rule. The powers of the two Assemblies were strictly limited but permitted some significant policy differences to emerge in fields such as health care. In two respects Labour promises in opposition were kept in a form that inverted their original meaning. One was the promise to replace the unelected and largely hereditary House of Lords with an elected second chamber. In practice, in 1999 the voting rights of all but 92 hereditary peers were removed, a handful of new life peers were appointed, and the issue of election was then in effect postponed indefinitely. The other promise made in opposition that was more or less reversed in practice was Labour's Freedom of Information Act, finally passed in 2000, whose list of exclusions appeared on balance to narrow public access to information rather than extend it. A third constitutional promise was to hold a referendum on whether the electoral system should be changed to make it 'fairer'. This promise was watered down, first by deferring a referendum until after the next general election, and then by planning to limit the choice to one between the existing system and the Alternative Vote (which has no proportional consequences), and finally abandoned.

should be the first political institutions to feel its effects, and should undergo a mutation fully as radical as their nineteenth century transformation into mass organisations following the extension of the franchise. The fundamental problem they faced was how to continue to be effective vote-winning organisations while following an increasingly corporate agenda.

The British Conservative Party had long had a mass membership, but it was essentially a 'party of notables' in which power rested both formally and in practice with its MPs. On this basis it had succeeded in governing the UK for most of the previous century and a half by successive adaptations of the interests of property to the demands of other classes.[52] But when Mrs Thatcher broke with the party's pragmatic tradition and declared herself a 'conviction politician', crusading for 'the free market and the strong state', the class alliance at the apex of this structure broke up. The 'Tory' elements in the party leadership were progressively displaced by free-market fundamentalist newcomers. The rural 'shires' lost their time-honoured precedence, and the divisions of interest within capital (finance vs. manufacturing, importers vs. exporters, small businesses vs. transnational corporations), instead of being mediated through national compromises struck within the party's inner circle, as in the past, were exacerbated by the new exposure to global competition.*

These divisions soon became focussed on the issue of Britain's relationship with Europe. Formed to encourage closer political union through freer trade, in the era of globalisation the EC/EU acquired an ambiguous significance, with a potential – however limited in practice so far – to regulate capital in the interests of European citizens rather than only in the interests of capitalists. The Thatcherite wing of the party was therefore hostile, but since by the

---

* Much was made at the time of the fact that the average age of Conservative Party members was 62 and there seemed no early likelihood of large-scale renewal. But with hindsight it is clear that since modern elections are fought largely through the media, large numbers of members are less important than large amounts of money.

1990s the EU accounted for 60 per cent of UK exports this conflicted with the party's ties to firms in the export sector. The EU's adoption of a single currency in 1999 aggravated the problem. Divisions over Europe played a large part in the party's 1997 election defeat. The more pragmatic, 'Tory' wing of the parliamentary party shrank through resignations and retirement, and by 2000 Conservative MPs were predominantly neoliberal and neoconservative ideologues who seemed unaware of the extent to which public opinion had moved away from the crusading neoliberalism of the Thatcher years; they looked likely to condemn the party to opposition indefinitely unless – or rather until – the Labour government self-destructed. William Hague, who succeeded John Major as Conservative leader in 1997, changed the party's constitution to give more power to the membership in the selection of the party leader, hoping to offset the influence of the party faithful against the warring factions of Conservative MPs, but if anything this compounded the problem. Even in 2006, when Labour was visibly imploding and a youthful new Conservative leader, David Cameron, had been elected, internal party divisions remained acute within the Conservative Party. The balancing act to be performed when the party returned to office promised to be extremely difficult.

The Labour Party, by contrast, had originally been a mass party, formed by and dependent on the trade union movement. Its leadership had always tried to portray it as representing the national interest, as opposed to the interests of the working class alone, seeking middle class support for measures to limit the impact of market forces on people's lives, chiefly through mildly progressive taxation and the pursuit of full employment along with state-provided social security, housing, education and health services. But after four successive election defeats (in 1979, 1983, 1987 and 1992) the 'modernisers' led by Blair had concluded that the 'new reality' of the global economy meant that to be elected they must accept Thatcher's legacy virtually in its entirety. Most of the party's activists were desperate enough to support almost anything that promised to end Conservative rule, but it was very doubtful if they would go on feeling this way if the leadership continued with Conservative policies once they were in office. The modernisers therefore took great pains to impress on the financial markets that party policy was now determined by the leader and a few close colleagues alone, and set about re-writing the party constitution to disempower not only the rank and file members and the trade unions but also, in effect, Labour MPs. The annual conference and the national executive were reconstructed to exclude potential challenges from below on policy issues. Leadership control was extended to the selection of candidates for election to parliament, the Scottish parliament, the Welsh Assembly, and the European Parliament. Members of the Shadow Cabinet – and later, even Cabinet Ministers – were required to clear all their speeches with the leader's office.[53] 'New Labour' (as Blair and his team now called the party) converged with the Conservative Party in its central organising principle.

New Labour also faced new contradictions, mirroring those of the Conservatives. To distance itself not just formally but in reality from the trade unions the party needed alternative sources of funds. It turned to rich donors attracted by its new, 'market-friendly' but socially moderate policy stance, but this not only exposed the party to the suspicion of selling influence but also called for policies that further alienated the trade unions – for instance, retaining virtually all of the Conservatives' industrial relations legislation and introducing a legal minimum wage at a level far below what the unions had hoped for. It also risked a serious loss of support among disillusioned 'old' Labour voters, and a loss of members who felt they were no longer part of the party's policy-making process, helping to carry forward the party's historic socialist project – a motivation that had worked very effectively, in spite of the very real limits to rank and file influence that existed under the old party constitution. And the degree of control that the leadership imposed over Labour's 'message', as it tried to square all these circles, had its own cost in the eventual reaction of journalists and the public against incessant 'spin'.

But what is at issue here is not the electoral prospects of either party, caught in the contradiction between the interests of global capital and the wishes of the electorate, but what the kind of party organisation that has now been adopted by both Labour and the Conservatives in response to this contradiction implies for democracy. To put it plainly, politics are no longer about managing the economy to satisfy the demands of voters, they are increasingly about getting voters to endorse policies that meet the demands of capital. The party leader's task is to adjust policy to the pressures of market forces, and to use every available means to secure consent for this, as free as possible from all encumbrances of doctrine and constraints of faction. Necessary for this purpose are people skilled in image construction and information management and the conduct of attitude surveys and focus groups. Party politics have become, in Polito's apt formulation, a 'realm of hyper-politics, where politics is exclusively concerned with itself', 'a daily struggle to win the attention of a public which has its mind on other matters' and in which 'the *software* of politics becomes decisive, its ability to adjust itself... to the country's state of mind, to intercept and encourage its moods.'[54]

Peter Mandelson, Labour's election campaign manager in 1997, told the Institute of Directors in 1998 that

> it had been the job of New Labour's architects to translate their understanding of the customer into offerings he or she was willing to pay for. And then, and only then, to convey to potential customers the attributes of that offering through all the different components that make up a successful brand – product positioning, packaging, advertising and communications.[55]

Absent from this model is any idea that a party represents ideals, or even interests, on the basis of which voters may be appealed to and against which policies will be judged. Preferences are assumed to be given, though 'volatile', and the task of the party leadership is to discover what they are and then try to make the chosen response to the 'new reality' of globalised markets appear to be in conformity with them.

A new breed of politicians emerges, adapted to this new kind of political management and to the new relationship with business demanded by the drastically altered balance of power between the state and private capital. Increasingly, they are full-time professional politicians, entering politics as young graduates employed as researchers for MPs or think tanks and without any experience in the wider workplace, or any significant history of involvement in grassroots party activity in which a taste for democratic practices might be acquired. As ministers in charge of government departments which outsource more and more of their work to private companies, they also rely heavily on 'outside' advice. Thousands of private sector consultants, costing the government well over £2 billion a year, have become a central feature of government, with little or no accountability for their often breath-taking failures.[56] Moreover government responsibilities that are not outsourced are increasingly entrusted to businessmen seconded to government departments from the private sector, while the flow of civil servants moving into corporate boardrooms also increases. A clear boundary between the state, as guardian of the public interest, and the private sector, which looks after private interests, was a cardinal principle of liberal and social democratic government in the past. In the textbooks of the 'New Public Management' it is no longer seen as a particular virtue. The 'revolving door' between the top echelons of the state and private enterprise becomes a state institution in itself.

The problem of party funding also pushes politicians further into the arms of capital. The more political success depends on opinion polling, focus groups and television, the more money parties need. But the less party members are allowed to influence (or even debate) policy, the fewer party members or activists there are and the less funding is available from membership subscriptions.

The Conservatives have always relied on donations from rich people. Now cultivating wealthy individuals has become normal for Labour too, predictably resulting in scandals.* The business lobby has become more and more intimately installed in Whitehall, while party membership has declined precipitously, as has electoral turnout, falling from 71 per cent of eligible voters in 1979 to 60 per cent in 2005.

Colin Crouch has perceptively summed up the new politics in an essay on what he calls 'post-democracy' referring to the fact that some residues from the relatively democratic era after the Second World War still co-exist with the market-driven politics produced by economic globalisation. Democracy thrives, Crouch suggests, 'when there are major opportunities for the mass of ordinary people to participate, through discussion and autonomous organisations, in shaping the agenda of public life....'. In post-democracy, by contrast,

> while elections certainly exist and can change governments, public electoral debate is a tightly controlled spectacle, managed by rival teams of professionals expert in the techniques of persuasion, and considering a small range of issues selected by those teams. The mass of citizens plays a passive, quiescent, even apathetic part, responding only to the signals given them. Behind this spectacle of the electoral game, politics is really shaped in private by interaction between

---

* Similar scandals over the way party funding has been acquired have afflicted one European party leader after another in recent years – Kohl in Germany, Chirac in France, Berlusconi in Italy, Blair in Britain. But only in Britain, characteristically, have the media focused not on the influence over policy that rich businessmen get in return for party funding, but on the fact that the quid pro quo may have been 'honours' – to be given a 'peerage' and become a 'lord' (or at least a 'knight'), in a repeat of the scandal precipitated by the sale of peerages by the Liberal prime minister Lloyd George at the end of the First World War. One might well wish that the chief executives and chairmen of Halliburton and Enron and the other companies which funded the Bush administration's electoral campaigns could have been so easily satisfied, instead of insisting that Bush refuse to ratify the Kyoto Protocol, drill for oil in nature reserves, privatize medicare, etc. In Britain the only alternative solution envisaged for the problem of financing parties of the new type was to fund party expenditure out of tax revenues. Since taxes are now rather regressive the government of capital, for capital and increasingly by capital would then be largely paid for by the workers, a fitting irony.

elected governments and elites that overwhelmingly represent business interests.[57]

Whether this is an 'exaggeration' of the situation that actually exists today, as Crouch rather cautiously suggests, may be doubted. At least in the case of Britain it is hard not to feel that it is a rather accurate summary. Either way, Crouch's conclusions on the kind of party that 'post-democracy' really requires are particularly interesting:

> If we extrapolate from recent trends, the classic party of the twenty-first century would be one which comprises a self-reproducing inner elite, remote from its mass movement, but nested squarely within a number of corporations, which will in turn fund the... opinion polling, policy-advice and vote-gathering services...[58]

And one 'almost pure example' of such a party already exists, Crouch suggests: Berlusconi's Forza Italia, which is essentially a network of companies owned by Berlusconi (including a near monopoly of the broadcast media), in which the political work needed for electoral success is done largely by his companies' employees.

Forza Italia, it is true, emerged under somewhat exceptional circumstances. But less 'pure' examples have long existed in the USA, as the Labour Party's 'modernisers' perceived, taking Bill Clinton's Democratic Party as the model to be emulated and sending their staffers to Washington to study its philosophy and techniques. They would obviously have indignantly rejected Engels' description of the American parties as 'two great gangs of political speculators'.[59] But to anyone contemplating the open ties between George W. Bush and the companies and sectors, from oil and defence to pharmaceuticals and health insurance, that have funded his campaigns and been the signal beneficiaries of his policies at home and abroad – not to mention the privately-owned media that have endorsed his lies – Engels' description is bound to seem rather accurate. The reality is that Forza Italia and the Republicans and Democrats are simply variant models of what 'democracy' must eventually come to mean everywhere in a neoliberal world. As Marx said to his German readers, in case they thought what was happening in England in the nineteenth century need not concern them: *de te fabula narratur* – it's you I'm talking about.[60]

Endnotes

1 Karl Polanyi, *The Great Transformation; the Political and Economic Origins of Our Time* (Beacon Press 1957 [1944]), p. 73.

2 Eric Hobsbawm, *Age of Extremes; The Short Twentieth Century 1914– 1991* (Abacus, 1995), p. 15.

3. David Held et al., *Global Transformations* (Stanford University Press, 1999), pp. 204-08. On derivatives and risk see Adam Tickell, 'Unstable Futures: Controlling and Creating Risks in International Money', in Leo Panitch and Colin Leys (eds.), *Global Capitalism Versus Democracy: Socialist Register 1999* (Merlin Press, 1999), pp. 248-77.

4 Peter Gowan, *The Global Gamble: Washington's Faustian Bid for World Dominance* (Verso, 1999), pp. 95-100.

5 John M. Stopford and Susan Strange, *Rival States, Rival Firms; Competition for World Market Shares* (Cambridge University Press, 1991), p. 15; Peter Dicken, *Global Shift* (Paul Chapman, second edition 1992), p. 57. The proportions of the various commodity markets controlled by TNCs were: over 80 percent, wheat, maize, coffee, cocoa, tea, pineapples, forest products, cotton, tobacco, jute, copper, iron ore, bauxite; 70-80 percent, rice, bananas, natural rubber, crude petroleum, tin; 50-70 percent, sugar, phosphates.

6 *World Investment Report 1993* (Paris, UNCTAD 1993), pp. 130 and 134.

7 Held et al., *Global Transformations*, p. 247.

8 Francois Chesnais, 'Globalisation, World Oligopoly and Some of Their Implications', in Marc Humbert (ed.), *The Impact of Globalisation on Europe's Firms and Industries* (Pinter, 1993), pp. 15-16.

9 Susan Strange, 'The Defective State', in *What Future for the State?*: *Daedalus* 124/2,1995, p. 59.

10 Chesnais ('Globalisation', p. 17) thinks that 'the entry of the Japanese keiretsu as major competitors in the late 1970s and their large-scale

penetration through investment into the US economy gave the onset of global oligopoly its irreversible character and made international cross-investment an imperative strategy for the survival of large firms'. On 'networks' see also Gunther Teubner, 'The Many-Headed Hydra: Networks as Higher-Order Collective Actors', in Joseph McCahery, Sol Piciotto and Colin Scott (eds.), *Corporate Control and Accountability* (Clarendon Press, 1993), pp. 41-60.

11 A 'back-of-the-envelope calculation' by the editors of the *Economist* cited in Barnet and Cavanagh, *Global Dreams*, p. 423.

12 Ibid., p. 135.

13 *World Investment Report* 1999, p. 6.

14 Dicken, *Global Shift*, p. 49. Of the world's 100 largest TNCs in 1992, 29 were American, 16 were Japanese, and 44 European (*World Investment Report* 1994, p. 8).

15 *World Investment Report* 1999, p. 17. Britain was twice as dependent on foreign TNCs as France, and three times as dependent as Germany or Italy. All the other comparably 'transnational' economies were much smaller.

16 George Monbiot, *Captive State; The Corporate Takeover of Britain* (Macmillan, 2000), pp. 188-89.

17 Susan Strange, 'The Name of the Game', in N.X. Rizopoulos (ed.), *Sea-Changes: American Foreign Policy in a World Transformed* (Council on Foreign Relations, 1990), p. 247; Barnet and Cavanagh, *Global Dreams*, p. 386; *Guardian*, 30 January 1996.

18 For instance Vivien A. Schmidt, writing about the European Union, notes that 'business' privileged access to supranational decision-making ensures that policy interactions have shifted from an almost exclusive reliance on national government bargaining [i.e. bargaining between the member governments] to one that includes, if it is not dominated by, business actors in the transnational sector' ('The New World Order, Incorporated', in *What Future for the State*, op. cit., p. 80).

19 Susan Strange, 'Rethinking Structural Change in the International Political Economy: States,Firms and Diplomacy', in Richard Stubbs and Geoffrey R.D. Underhill (eds.), *Political Economy and the Changing Global Order* (Macmillan, 1994), p. 111.

20 The company later merged with Glaxo to become Glaxo SmithKline. See Monbiot, *Captive State*, pp. 254-61.

21 Teubner, 'The Many-Headed Hydra', p. 58, quoting H. Collins, 'Ascription of Legal Responsibility in Complex Patterns of Economic Integration', 53 *Modern Law Review* 1990, p. 731.

22 Sol Picciotto, 'Transfer Pricing and Corporate Regulation', in McCahery et al., *Corporate Control*, p. 387. Picciotto's major study, *International Business Taxation* (Clarendon Press, 1992) describes in dispassionate detail the elaborate ways corporations avoid tax, and the hitherto rather ineffectual responses of international cooperation between tax authorities.

23 Michael Wallerstein and Adam Przeworski, 'Capital Taxation With Open Borders', *Review of International Political Economy* 2/3, 1995, 425-45. The authors criticise the view that this flowed necessarily from capital mobility, arguing that provided the full cost of investment is tax deductible, as it usually is, only fear of tax changes, and not the absolute level of tax on profits, affects investment flows.

24 Anthony Ginsberg, quoted in Barnet and Cavanagh, *Global Dreams*, p. 389. In a survey of the capital income tax situation in the EC in the early 1990s, Peter B. Sorenson concluded: 'Governments in Europe should seriously consider whether they wish to retain personal taxes on income from capital in reality and not just on paper… If EC governments refuse to face this challenge directly, the days of the personal income tax as we know it may be numbered' ('Coordination of Capital and Income Taxes in the Economic and Monetary Union: What Needs to Be Done?', in Francisco Torres and Francesco Giavazzi (eds.), *Adjustment and Growth in the European Monetary Union* (Cambridge University Press, 1993), p. 378. The problem remains largely unaddressed.

25 Ben Steil, 'Competition, Integration and Regulation in EC Capital Markets', in Cable and Henderson (eds.), *Trade Blocs?*, p. 155.

26 Hamish Macrae, '1960s Financial Markets', *The World in 1996*, Economist Publications 1996, pp. 124 and 127.

27 Philip G. Cerny (ed.), *Finance and World Markets: Markets, Regimes and States in the Post-hegemonic Era* (Edward Elgar, 1993), pp. 79-80.

28 Timothy J. Sinclair, 'Passing Judgment; Credit Rating Processes as Regulatory Mechanisms of Governance in the Emerging World Order', *Review of International Political Economy* 1/1, 1994, pp. 133-59.

Whether the credit agencies or their clients always make intelligent use of the data they collect may be doubted, in view of the failure to foresee either the Mexican crisis of 1994 or the East Asian crisis of 1997-98, but this does not make their political influence less significant.

29 For a discussion of proposals concerning pension funds see e.g. Robin Blackburn, 'The New Collectivism: Pension Reform, Grey Capitalism and Complex Socialism', *New Left Review* I/233, 1999, pp.3-65, and the subsequent exchange between Blackburn and Henri Jacot in *New Left Review* II/1 2000, pp. 122-36.

30 In a study of 15 countries from 1967 to 1990 Garrett found that 'the financial markets always attached interest rate premia to the power of the left and organized labor' and that these premia appeared to increase with greater capital mobility. 'Presumably, these results reflect the market's skepticism about the willingness of governments to pursue "prudent" macroeconomic policies where the left and organized labor are powerful' ('Capital Mobility, Trade, and Domestic Politics', in Robert O. Keohane and Helen V. Milner (eds.), *Internationalization and Domestic Politics* [Cambridge University Press, 1996], p. 95).

31 Held et al., *Global Transformations*, p. 165, citing S. Page, *How Countries Trade* (London: Routledge, 1994), Chapter 4.

32 John H. Dunning, *Globalization: The Challenge for National Economic Regimes* (Economic and Social Research Institute, Dublin, 1993), p. 15.

33 Jeanne-Mey Sun and Jacques Pelkmans, 'Regulatory Competition in the Single Market', *Journal of Common Market Studies* 33/1, 1955, pp. 67-89.

34 On the creation of millionaires by corporate executive stock options see Wally Seccombe, 'Contradictions of Shareholder Capitalism: Downsizing Jobs, Enlisting Savings, Destabilising Families', in Panitch and Leys (eds.), *Socialist Register 1999*, pp. 76-107. Data on the numbers of millionaires and billionaires are produced by Merrill Lynch and Capgemini in annual World Wealth Reports. The 793 billionaires counted in 2006 were said to own $2.6 trillion between them.

35 Cable notes the emergence in the older industrial countries of what used to be the hall-mark of 'third-world' societies: '... for the educated and moneyed section of the population, the opportunities presented by globalization – travel, wider experience, promotion – are great. We thus have one, potentially large, disadvantaged, alienated and powerless

element in society, and another which is flourishing but has less of a stake in the success of any particular country.' ('The Diminished Nation State', p. 43).

36 The Manifesto of the Communist Party, in Karl Marx, *The Revolutions of 1848* (Penguin, 1973), pp. 70-71.

37 *Social Trends 36*, 2000 edition (London: Office of National Statistics, 2000). Unless otherwise indicated the data in this and the two following paragraphs are from this and later editions of *Social Trends*.

38 The category 'manual work' was finally abandoned in government statistics by the end of the 1990s, as technical change and the feminization of work made it increasingly problematic.

39 Accurate data on the distribution of shareholding are essentially non-existent. According to *Social Trends* 30, 17 per cent of adults owned shares in 1998. According to the London Stock Exchange's *Facts on File 1999*, 24 million people owned shares. The latter figure seems to have been calculated by including the number of members of building societies who had received shares in them when their societies 'de-mutualised' and became banks. It seems likely that a high proportion of these shareholdings would have soon been disposed of. Nonetheless a gradually growing minority of people undoubtedly owned a small number of shares. Looked at the other way round, individual British shareholders owned between them about a quarter of all shares, while foreign shareholders owned another quarter and institutions a half.

40 For an only slightly excessive portrait of one of these, the once fashionable Lowestoft, see W. G. Sebald's *The Rings of Saturn* (London: The Harvill Press, 1998), pp. 40-48.

41 Christopher Hird, *Fulcrum Productions*, interview 2 December 1999.

42 David Saunders, 'Goodbye to All That', *Guardian*, 3 July 2000.

43 See Monbiot, *Captive State*, passim.

44 For the dependence of scientific research in universities on corporate funding see Monbiot, *Captive State*, chapter 9.

45 R. Jowell et al. (eds.), *The British Social Attitudes Survey, the 16th Report: Who Shares New Labour Values?* (Ashgate, 1999), pp. 25 and 28.

46 On the growth of PR in Britain see Aeron Davis, *Public Relations Democracy: Public Relations, Politics and the Mass Media in Britain* (Manchester: Manchester University Press, 2002).

47 Thanks to spending cuts elsewhere, higher unemployment, an ageing population, intensified work rates leading to more disability, etc., spending on social security nonetheless rose as a proportion of all government spending from just over 20 per cent in 1980 to nearly 40 per cent in 1999, offering an ever-larger target for the right in its unrelenting call for cuts in 'welfare'.

48 See the *Local Government Act, 2000*. In 1960, as an opposition backbencher, Margaret Thatcher had promoted a law that opened councils up to public scrutiny as a means of limiting corruption, real or alleged, in Labour-controlled councils. The difference that the globalisation years had made to both parties' attitudes to democracy is instructive.

49 Stuart Weir and Wendy Hall (eds.), *EGO Trip: Extra-governmental Organisations in the United Kingdom and their Accountability* (The Scarman Trust for Democratic Audit, 1994); and Wendy Hall and Stuart Weir, *The Untouchables: Power and Accountability in the Quango State* (The Scarman Trust, 1996).

50 Michael Power, *The Audit Society: Rituals of Verification* (Oxford University Press, 1997), p. 3.

51 In an article in the *Daily Mail*, 26 March 1997. An alternative version appeared in Blair's foreword, as Prime Minister, to the 1998 White Paper on Employment Law: 'the most tightly regulated labour market of any leading economy in the world'.

52 On parties of notables see Maurice Duverger, *Political Parties: Their Organisation and Activity in the Modern State* (Methuen, 1954); also Andrew Gamble, *The Conservative Nation* (Routledge and Kegan Paul, 1974), and A. J. Davies, *We, the Nation: The Conservative Party and the Pursuit of Power* (Little, Brown, 1995).

53 The transformation of the Labour Party is the subject of an enormous literature. For a useful survey see Steve Ludlam, 'New Labour: What's Published is What Counts', *British Journal of Politics and International Relations*, 2/2, 2000, pp. 264-76. For the changes in Labour's constitution see Leo Panitch and Colin Leys, *The End of Parliamentary Socialism*, 2nd edition (Verso, 2001), Chapters 10 and 13.

54 A. Polito, *Cool Britannia: Gli Inglezi (E Gli Italiani) Visti di Londra* (Donzelli, 1998), cited in Eric Hobsbawm, 'The Death of Neo-Liberalism', *Marxism Today*, November-December 1998, pp. 4-8.

55 *Guardian*, 30 April 1998. If Mandelson was joking it is not recorded that his audience noticed it. The previous year, just after the election, he had told a meeting in Germany that 'ballot boxes and Parliaments were elitist relics' and that people wanted to be more 'involved in government' through 'the far superior instruments of plebiscites, focus groups and the internet... It may be that the era of pure representative democracy is coming to an end.' The Germans were not amused (Nick Cohen, 'New Labour... in Focus, on Message, out of Control', *Observer*, 28 November 1999).

56 *Guardian*, 2 September 2006. The extraordinary scale of the use of consultants, and the extraordinary deception and waste involved, is documented by David Craig in *Plundering the Public Sector: How New Labour are Letting Consultants Run off with £70 Billion of Our Money*, London: Constable and Robinson, 2006.

57 Colin Crouch, *Post-Democracy* (Cambridge: Polity Press, 2004), pp. 2-4.

58 Ibid., p. 74.

59 Friedrich Engels, Introduction to *The Civil War in France*, in Robert C. Tucker, *The Marx-Engels Reader* (Norton, 1978), p. 627.

60 Karl Marx, Preface to the First Edition of *Capital*, Vol. I (Penguin Books, 1978), p. 90.

The Cynical State

Mendacity is a system that we live in. (Tennessee Williams, *Cat on a Hot Tin Roof*)

Governments have always lied. They naturally deny it, even long after it is abundantly clear that they have lied, trailing multiple red herrings, dismissing inconvenient evidence, implying that there is counter-evidence they are not free to produce. When a lie can no longer be credibly denied it is justified, usually by an appeal to the national interest. Governments of modern representative democracies are no different, even if they are more liable than dictators to be exposed. Half-truths and outright lies are routinely told. Facts are routinely concealed. Files are unaccountably lost. Tapes are mysteriously erased. Democratic checks and balances are rarely effective and the public's collective memory is short.

Even so, in recent years state cynicism has broken new ground. The British government's flagrant abuse of military intelligence to persuade parliament and the public to endorse its attack on Iraq was a dramatic case in point. In July 2003, soon after the official end of the war, a British government weapons expert, David Kelly, killed himself after being revealed as the source for a BBC report that the government's dossier outlining the intelligence had been knowingly 'sexed up'. The government appointed a reliable judge, Lord Hutton, to hold a public enquiry into Kelly's death. The evidence given to the enquiry showed that the Prime Minister's staff had been working flat out to make it appear that Saddam Hussein posed a threat to Britain that would justify invading Iraq. The government's intelligence 'dossier' was made to read much more alarmingly than the evidence produced by the intelligence services warranted. It claimed that Iraq had nerve gases, anthrax spores, ricin, botulinium toxin, mobile laboratories, nuclear materials and extended range rockets, none of which the intelligence service claimed as facts, and none of which later proved to be true. It also claimed several times that Iraq had weapons of mass destruction 'deployable within 45 minutes'. This claim was known to be vague, from an uncorroborated second-hand source, and to refer only to 'battlefield' weapons; and it too proved entirely unfounded. But more than any other piece of false information it was decisive in securing parliamentary and public acquiescence in the attack on Iraq.

The defence minister, Geoff Hoon, admitted to the Hutton enquiry that he knew the report referred only to battlefield weapons, not the long-distance missiles that most people assumed were meant by the expression 'weapons of mass destruction'. When asked why he had not corrected press reports that made this assumption he said his experience showed that correcting incorrect press reports was unprofitable. He was not challenged on this, or pressed to comment on the influence these reports had had on public opinion, although the record showed that the prime minister's staff were intently focused on ensuring that press headlines would be as alarming as possible. The evidence also showed that Hoon, Blair, and Blair's chief press officer Alastair Campbell had all subsequently told further lies about the compilation of the dossier. Campbell told Hutton that he had had no input into the dossier. The evidence showed he had had extensive input. Hoon told the parliamentary committee on defence that he had had nothing to do with it either. The evidence showed he had been involved as much as anyone. Most famously, Blair told the House of Commons that it was 'completely and totally untrue' that there was disquiet in the intelligence community over the 45-minute claim, but a senior intelligence officer told the enquiry that he and one of his colleagues had submitted a written report about their disquiet.[1]

Of course commentators who supported the attack on Iraq were willing to condone all this. But Lord Hutton condoned it absolutely too. The only behaviour he criticized in his final report was that of Andrew Gilligan, the BBC journalist who had broken the story, and the BBC director general and chairman who had backed him against furious attacks by the Prime Minister's office. All of them were forced to resign, while Blair and Hoon were totally absolved. John Scarlett, the senior intelligence official who had agreed to 'sex up' the intelligence service's original draft of the dossier at the behest of the Prime Minister's office, was promoted to be head of the secret service.[2] What is more, Hutton's decision to put all the evidence on the internet, but then to condemn the whistleblowers and exonerate the liars, meant that members of parliament and the electorate were being asked to become complicit in official mendacity. 'Transparent' government, he seemed to say, just means that MPs and voters must accept being lied to and that no one should be penalized for doing so.

As the occupation of Iraq dragged on, its apologists' indifference to the facts became more and more insulting to the intelligence of the public. In March 2005 Gary Younge, a usually restrained commentator, summed up the general sense of disgust: 'We have entered a world where reality... is just a minor blockage in a flood of official, upbeat declarations... Each new dispatch from the departments of irony on both sides of the Atlantic suggests that truth can be created by assertion...'.[3]

Dissimulation is, of course, part of war, even if lying to your own electorate is a negation of democracy. But a cynical indifference to the truth is now hardly less common in domestic policy. For instance, in the Labour government's determination to 'marketize' health care it has shown itself equally willing to use flawed evidence. An article published in the authoritative *British Medical Journal* (BMJ) purported to show that an American Health Maintenance Organization or HMO, Kaiser Permanente, was more efficient than the National Health Service. The medical research community around the world immediately denounced the study as hopelessly flawed.[4] The government, however, adopted Kaiser Permanente as a model for the NHS to follow – citing it in policy documents and inviting Kaiser staff to advise the Department of Health.[5]

Another example was the government's decision to adopt a programme called 'Evercare' operated by another American HMO, United Healthcare. United Healthcare claimed that Evercare reduced the rate of emergency hospitalisation of frail elderly people by 50 per cent. United Healthcare had a notorious record of health care fraud in the USA, but its CEO gave $1.5 million to the 2004 Bush-Cheney election campaign and Bush's secretary for health recommended the company to the British secretary of state for health. In 2004 Simon Stevens, Blair's senior health policy adviser, resigned to become United Healthcare's new President for Europe and secured a contract to introduce Evercare in Britain. A study of nine pilot schemes in the UK costing £3.4 million, however, showed that Evercare was unlikely to cut the rate of hospitalization by more than 1 per cent. Yet the government's primary care 'czar' declared that 'there is nothing in the research to make us have second thoughts about the strategy'.[6]

These stories, which could be replicated for almost any field of public policy in contemporary Britain, illustrate the emergence of a new, neoliberal policy regime that is more brazenly willing to dissemble, more indifferent to evidence, more aggressive towards critics and distinctly less accountable – to the point of being virtually unaccountable – than ever before. This policy regime is not peculiarly British. The old 'liberal/social democratic' policy regime which it has displaced did have distinctively British features. The new neoliberal policy regime is a more standardized affair. It not only spans the Atlantic but thanks to neoliberal globalization it is being gradually replicated, in essentials, throughout the world. Its key feature is that policy is now fundamentally about national competitiveness and responding to global market forces. The crucial roles are played neither by political parties nor by civil servants but personnel seconded into the civil service from the private sector, a handful of 'special advisers' to the prime minister, a small group of certified market-friendly civil servants, and polling, advertising and media experts. Scientific evidence is still relied on, but only in so far as it serves competition policy; otherwise it is treated uncritically, if it helps the government, and dismissed if it does not. When this new policy regime is properly understood the lies about Iraq no longer appear as a special case, but only as a special dimension of a general one. Cynicism, we realize, is a necessary condition of neoliberal democracy.

The liberal/social democratic policy regime

Britain's previous liberal/social democratic policy regime combined elements of the Liberals' state reforms of the late nineteenth century with elements corresponding to the interventionist state of the twentieth. The Liberals created a higher civil service recruited competitively from the cleverest members of the same social class, and educated at the same elite private schools and universities, as the elected ministers they served. The idea was that officials of this calibre and background would be in a position to offer elected ministers honest advice and 'to some extent influence' them, in a shared 'freemasonry' of public service.[7] Because the emphasis was on social and political status, higher civil servants were, like almost all the ministers they served, 'generalists', relying for expertise on the advice of professional and technical civil servants – engineers, public health doctors, biologists, etc. For dealing with big issues of a politically sensitive nature they would recommend the establishment of Royal Commissions composed of eminent experts with powers to commission research and call for expert evidence (between 1950 and 1980 one was appointed, on average, almost every year).

For lesser issues that nonetheless called for additional expertise a Departmental Enquiry could be set up, also with powers to draw on outside expertise.

With the advent of the Labour Party and an increasingly interventionist state agenda other elements were added to the mix. Innovating parties needed to develop policies out of office to present to the civil service when elected. The Labour Party had a research department that produced blueprints for new policies, as did the Trade Union Congress and the larger trade unions. The Fabian Society, established in 1884 with the aim of 'permeating' the main governing parties, became more and more linked to Labour and supplied it with a steady flow of reasonably well worked-out policy proposals. PEP (Political and Economic Planning), founded in 1931, and NIESR (the National Institute of Economic and Social Research), founded in 1938, were products of the depression and aimed in different ways to push social and economic reforms of a broadly liberal/social-democratic nature by publishing serious research on the issues. From 1929 onwards the Conservative Party also had a research department. Many leading politicians, from Cripps and Wilson to Macmillan and Heath, were intellectuals, often former academics and frequently authors of books and pamphlets on policy issues. The civil service existed to advise governments on the policy initiatives derived from all these sources, and turn them into practical plans and laws.

There were differences and tensions between the state and non-state components of this policy regime, but they shared a general commitment to a notion of objectivity, in the sense that policy proposals should be judged on the basis of rational argument and sound evidence. They all saw themselves as professionals, belonging to a 'public' domain, serving the public interest.

> The public domain... was quintessentially the domain of... professionals. Professional pride, professional competence, professional duty, professional authority and, not least, predictable professional career paths were of its essence. Professionals were the

chief advocates of its growth; they managed most of its institutions, and they policed the frontier between it and the adjacent private and market domains. Above all, the values of the public domain were their values.[8]

The central tension in the liberal/democratic policy regime in the 1950s and '60s was due to the fact that the higher civil service, and especially its elite in the Treasury, which exercised considerable control over other departments' policies, was more inclined to be liberal than social-democratic. Moreover the 'freemasonry' which Gladstone's reforms had postulated between the higher civil service and ministers began to show cracks once the ministers were Labour MPs, with ideas and aims reflecting the party's roots in the labour movement and no longer predominantly educated at leading private schools or at Oxford or Cambridge.

Thomas Balogh, an economic adviser to the Labour prime minister Harold Wilson in the 1960s, voiced a growing impatience with the higher civil service's typically humanities-based education and pre-industrial social attitudes, denouncing it as 'the apotheosis of the dilettante'.[9] In 1966 Wilson created a Department of Economic Affairs to offset what was seen as the Treasury's bias for financial prudence over economic growth, and a Treasury departmental committee chaired by Lord Fulton (a university vice-chancellor) recommended a reorganization of the higher civil service on technocratic lines. A Civil Service College was established, to emulate the French École Nationale d'Administration, and a Civil Service Department took over the Treasury's management of recruitment, training and promotion.

Almost all these initiatives were neutralized, largely by the higher civil service itself. The Department of Economic Affairs was closed in 1969 after only three years. The Civil Service Department lasted longer, but was closed by Mrs. Thatcher in 1981. The Civil Service College survives, but only as a provider of short courses, with no prestige. The one significant innovation of the Wilson years that not only survived but flourished was the increased use of 'special advisers', brought in from outside to bolster ministers in the face of what was seen as excessive civil service caution or conservatism. The Fulton Report had also recommended this, together with 'greater mobility between [the civil service] and other employments', including 'temporary appointments for fixed periods, short-term interchanges of staff and freer movement out of the Service', and giving further thought to 'hiving off' activities to non-departmental organizations. All of this prefigured the erosion of the boundaries between the public and private domains that was to take place under the neoliberal policy regime from the 1980s onwards.

But in retrospect it is easy to see that the issue was not merely changing class relations, or generalists versus technocrats; the fundamental tension within the old policy regime was the contradiction of social democracy itself. The real problem was that by the end of the 1960s British trade unions were unwilling to see the problems of British capitalism solved at their expense, while capitalists were unwilling to collaborate in any state-led economic strategy so long as the unions remained powerful, as even the Conservative prime minister Edward Heath discovered to his chagrin after taking office in 1970. (In 1973 he told a meeting of the Institute of Directors: 'When we came in we were told that there weren't sufficient inducements to invest, so we provided the inducements. Then we were told people were scared of balance of payments difficulties leading to stop-go. So we floated the pound. Then we were told of fears of inflation; and now we're dealing with that. And still you aren't investing enough!')[10]

The crisis came to a head in the winter of 1973-74. With the coal-miners 'working to rule' and the entire country limited to a three-day working week to conserve fuel, the head of the civil service, William Armstrong, had a nervous breakdown. The liberal/social democratic policy regime had collapsed. 'From that moment', Peter Gowan noted in a seminal article, 'a current within the Conservative Party... [was] working to make... [the Gladstonian civil service model] redundant by removing labour as a major force on the political scene, Americanizing the party system and state bureaucracy and breaking up the mandarinate.[11]

The Labour Party returned to office in 1974 but crisis management became the overriding agenda. Domestic policy initiatives, from any source, were irrelevant unless they helped meet the conditions attached to the IMF loan that the Treasury mandarins and the Labour leadership decided they must accept, rather than embrace the socialist alternative advocated by the Labour Party's left wing. The IMF's conditions meant replacing Keynesianism by monetarism, opening the door to Thatcherism and the construction of a new, neoliberal policy regime.

The transition to a neoliberal policy regime

The starting-point for understanding the new policy regime is the ascendancy of capital that followed – and was meant to follow – from Thatcher's and Reagan's elimination of controls on cross-border capital movements from the early 1980s onwards. This allowed the financial markets and transnational corporations to set increasingly tight limits on the policies national governments could adopt.[12] These limits were registered in the political 'risk premium' that the markets placed on any government seen as liable to adopt policies – on taxation, on government spending, on labour regulation or environmental protection, etc. – that would reduce the profitability of capital, compared with governments elsewhere. In Britain before the 1992 election the risk premium for a possible Labour government was 2 per cent. To reduce this to 0.5 per cent (which they managed to do before the 1997 election), the new Labour leadership scrapped virtually all Labour's 'market unfriendly' policy commitments, deleted Clause Four (which still talked of public ownership) from the party's constitution, and adopted a new range of policies called for by the City of London (the heart of the country's financial sector), including handing over the setting of interest rates to the independent Bank of England and adopting the

Conservatives' policy of having virtually all new public buildings financed and owned by the private sector.

Capital's political and social power had also been enormously increased by the Conservatives between 1979 and 1997, and Blair showed no inclination to challenge it. The chief executives of big companies continued to enjoy easy access to ministers and even the prime minister, and got respectful attention. This enabled them to overcome barriers intended to protect the public interest in one field after another – town planning legislation, GM food, the ownership of genes, the science research agenda of universities, etc. The trade unions, on the other hand, had been forced to accept an industrial relations regime that Tony Blair – who retained almost all of it – was pleased to call 'the most lightly regulated labour market of any leading economy in the world'.

The constantly-increasing power of capital also made private enterprise seem the natural order of things. Not only had Labour's post-war nationalizations been undone, from electricity and gas to public transport, but many services that had always been public, such as prisons and airports, were now privately owned and run, while cultural and sporting events (and even police forces) increasingly relied on corporate sponsors until every dimension of daily life was tagged with their logos.

'New' Labour's strategists, the so-called 'modernizers', saw all this as 'the new reality'. Their idea was to win and hold power by not just fully accepting the new reality but accepting it so whole-heartedly that there would be no room left on that terrain for the Conservative Party, which would become as 'unelectable' as Labour had been from 1979 to 1994. This strategy meant insulating the Labour leader from pressure from the trade unions and party members. So the party's constitution was rewritten and the annual conference emasculated as a policy-making (or even a policy-debating) forum. Of course the modernizers envisaged a 'third way', along which they would pursue whatever policies they considered progressive, in terms of what the new reality allowed; but they had no confidence that these would meet with the approval of the party rank and file and they were not disposed to have any public arguments about it.[13] Logically enough, too, the party's policy research capacity was also run down and eventually abolished. Blair declared that the party was now 'a party of business', and on that basis business could be asked to pay for whatever policy research the leadership wanted done.

Yet there was, obviously, still a need for policies – just within much narrower limits. With capital's freedom restored, the rules of policy-making changed. Major economic policies are still made, but in conformity with an overall agenda set by transnational corporations and the international and regional agencies they dominate. These *global market* policies involve adapting the British economy and Britain's socio-economic institutions (fiscal policy, aid to industry, education, training, the health and safety and labour market regulation, etc.) to compete successfully in the global marketplace. Since these policies are often electorally unpalatable they are made as far as possible out of the public eye – inside Whitehall or the European Commission, at the WTO – from where, once made, they appear as the impersonal and unavoidable effects of the market. 'Treasury control' – the time-honoured principle that all departmental policies involving spending must be pre-approved by the Treasury – has acquired a new significance. Now all major expenditures also have to serve the government's overall competition strategy.

All this meant that by the turn of the century it was only in the domain of *socio-cultural adjustment* policies that governments presented themselves in terms of having significant choices. Personal taxation, the scope and quality of public services, crime and 'security', immigration and 'identity politics' are the main terrains on which these policies are made. Here a wider range of options exists, but within limits that are broadly the same for all parties; and for much of this kind of policy-making it is pollsters, marketing experts and spin-doctors, as much as civil servants (let alone researchers), who are seen as having the required expertise to manage public opinion and adjust the electorate to the necessary consequences of global market policy-making. The two sorts of policy are of course interdependent, and give rise to politically awkward dilemmas. To keep wages down immigrants are required, but immigrants are the right wing press' favourite scapegoats for every social ill; social services are popular, but the regressive tax system insisted on by the markets means that paying for them is politically unpopular; and so on. So what is the nature of the new neoliberal policy-making regime that these conditions entail?

The neoliberal policy regime

First of all, the civil service has been radically reorganized on business lines, following the doctrines of the 'new public management'. As many activities as possible have been transferred out of government departments into 'executive agencies', leaving a reduced policy-related higher civil service at the top. The slimmed-down departments have then been further slimmed down to achieve 'efficiency savings', and required to 'outsource' more and more of their routine functions to private companies, starting with cleaning and continuing with information technology, accounting, estate management, personnel, and so on. Government buildings are sold and leased back from private companies. Sometimes individual public services, such as various prisons or schools, or even a whole local education authority, are directly outsourced to be run by private companies.

But the role of those remaining at the top has changed too. Thatcher's ministers made it clear that dispassionate advice and careful argument were out. When she took office and started taking an unprecedented interest (for a prime minister) in higher civil service promotions, the quality she looked for was a capacity for vigorous implementation of her ideas. Early on she got into an argument about industrial relations, about which she had strong opinions but was poorly informed, with Donald Derx, a capable and dedicated civil servant. She went on and on until Derx finally said: 'Prime Minister, do you really want to know the facts?' – and promptly ended his prospects of promotion.[14] As David Marquand says,

> ... civil servants were no longer expected to tell the truth to power... In a phrase coined by Lord Bancroft, head of the civil service when Mrs Thatcher came to power, the 'grovel count' rose sharply. Those who could not bring themselves to grovel languished or left. Inevitably, those who grovelled internalized the crucial axioms of the government's new ideology and statecraft.[15]

New Labour showed no inclination to change this. They too wanted civil servants to be as like businessmen as possible. Thatcher's ministers told civil servants that they didn't want 'whingeing, analysis or integrity, that we must do as we are told and that they have several friends in the private sector who could do the job in a morning with one hand tied behind their back'.[16] Twenty-five years later Blair was telling them the same thing: 'Rigour about performance must be at the heart of a leaner, more efficient civil service... A culture of decision-making by committee, while ensuring all possible viewpoints are considered, leads to unnecessary delays and increased cost'.[17] In 2005 the head of the civil service, Sir Andrew Turnbull, very much 'on message', told a conference that 'the upper civil service had been forced to refocus its efforts from policy and management to an active role in the delivery of targets and key services. "The job is much more akin to being a chief executive officer than it has been in the past", he admitted'.[18]

But if senior civil servants are no longer primarily concerned with making policy, who is? Definitely not Royal Commissions. To 'conviction' politicians, 'ensuring all possible viewpoints are considered' seems a pointless diversion from where they are convinced the country should go, and neither Thatcher nor Major appointed any Royal Commissions. In his first two years in office Blair appointed two, but rejected both their recommendations and never appointed another.[19] Even departmental enquiries, whose terms and proceedings can be much more closely controlled by ministers, have become relatively rare.[20] And policies emanating from party members and developed through internal party debates and compromises are definitely a thing of the past.

One obvious alternative source of policy-making that corresponds to this situation is 'think tanks', and it is certainly true that think tanks see themselves as playing a crucial policy-making role. But British think tanks are not the sort of intellectual powerhouse familiar in the USA, with massive private foundation funding.[21] Most British think tanks have only a handful of staff and budgets of a few hundred thousand pounds, and competition between them for funding – which is predominantly corporate – tends to make most of them more anxious to have media coverage than a reputation for serious research. As Andrew Denham and Mark Garnett note, it was Demos, 'the think tank with the flimsiest ideological attire' and a taste for 'back-of-an-envelope radicalism' (it first won attention with a pamphlet attacking the powers of the Queen) that most appealed to New Labour in office, and its founding director Geoff Mulgan went on to become head of Tony Blair's Cabinet Office Strategy Unit in 2003.[22] Even the more intellectually conventional Institute for Public Policy Research (IPPR), whose director Matthew Taylor became head of policy planning in the prime minister's Policy Directorate in 2003, appears lightweight, at least by comparison with the think tanks founded in response to the depression of the 1930s. Those earlier think tanks were 'at least… motivated by the hope that their findings would be educative, either for policy-makers or for the public. Even on a charitable view, this urge [now] seems lacking…'[23]

The characteristic claim of every new think tank is that there is a need for 'new ideas' – which indeed there is, since so many of the important ones have been ruled out as unacceptable to the market, or politically risky. The trouble is that in the narrow range that remains there are few useful new ideas to be had. Catherine Bennett summed up the problem perfectly in 2002:

If there is not already some sort of car boot sale where rejected or nearly-new thoughts can be bought, recycled, or exchanged for other unwanted policies, then it is high time one of the thinkers started one. With new tanks established almost daily, each one creating thousands of thoughts and papers, debates and alternative manifestos, each of which must be printed and circulated before it can be shelved, something has got to be done. Rubbish disposal experts estimate that getting rid of the IPPR's thought mountain, alone, already accounts for a landfill site the size of Croydon. Over at the government's Performance and Innovation Unit, John Birt's dedicated crater is said to be visible from space.[24]

The common overestimation of the influence of think tanks is largely due to the fact that in the run-up to Thatcher's accession to power in 1979, right-wing think tanks were an important source of neo-Conservative policy. From 1955 onwards the Institute of Economic Affairs (IEA) had served as a crucial base for 'organic intellectuals' of capitalism, sustaining and updating the strand of bourgeois thought that rejected the post-war compromise with social democracy. As Richard Cockett showed in his book *Thinking the Unthinkable*, when the contradictions of the post-war compromise finally brought it to an end, allowing Mrs Thatcher to capture the leadership of the Conservative Party in 1975 and win power in 1979, her principal lieutenants at first drew heavily on the work of the IEA as well as the new Centre for Policy Studies, founded in 1974, and the Adam Smith Institute, founded in 1977.[25] It was the apparent influence of these three think tanks during those years that prompted the Labour leadership to create the IPPR in 1988, while they were in opposition, the Liberal Democrats (also in opposition) to create the Social Market Foundation in 1989; and the New Labour 'modernizers', on the eve of their capture of the party leadership, to found Demos in 1993. And these in turn prompted the formation of a rapidly proliferating medley of imitators, left and right, all striving for a place in the councils of power. To quote Bennett again:

Once you add the product of all the other think tanks – Demos, Civitas, the Centre for Policy Studies, Localis, Policy Exchange, Reform, the Adam Smith Institute, NLGN, Politeia, the Foreign

Policy Centre, the Social Affairs Unit, Catalyst, the Fabian Society,
the Social Market Foundation, the racy new Do Tank and others
too numerous to list, you are forced to think the unthinkable: who
needs them?[26]

Who indeed? For the role played by the new right think tanks before
Thatcher's 1979 election victory could not be repeated after it. Once
neoliberal globalization had been accomplished, the scope for
radical policy-making was drastically narrowed. Think tanks, which
are not privy to much essential information about the global market
forces involved in the making of economic policy, and which also
depend on maximizing publicity to keep their funding coming in,
cannot contribute significantly to economic policy-making, least of
all for a party in office. That work must be done by true experts. Nor
are think tanks well suited to helping to make the ongoing social and
cultural policy adjustments that changing global markets require.
Pollsters and marketing experts are the key to success there.

From time to time the government will toy with an obvious
think-tank brain-child, such as 'citizenship ceremonies' for 18-year
olds – usually to universal derision. 'Baby bonds' – a pet IPPR project
for opening an account for every newborn infant into which the
government would put some money, to give everyone some cash
to do something with at 21 – did make it into Labour's pre-election
budget in 2005, though to no great effect, at least electorally. In spite
of their claims to the contrary it is hard to credit think tanks with
being the source of any significant New Labour policy initiative.[27]
Ministers and opposition leaders do use sympathetic think tanks
as sounding-boards, making speeches or writing pamphlets under
their auspices – which suggests that think tanks may do more to
make market-driven policies palatable to voters than to turn popular
sentiment into practicable policies.

Think tanks do serve as useful pools of political talent and
ambition. On taking office in 1997 the Labour government doubled
the number of ministers' 'special advisers' from 38 to 72, and many
come from the think-tanks clustered around Westminster. Few of

them bring relevant expertise from outside or carry intellectual weight inside. What most of them have is energy and a willingness to help work up solutions to whatever problems their minister is faced with. The key qualifications are loyalty and readiness to turn one's hand to whatever task is needed. Peter Hyman, a former special adviser to Tony Blair, says that a few advisers have their own ideas, which may be different from those of their ministers. But the 'vast majority', he reassures us, 'know they are there to serve the minister who employs them'.[28] Denham and Garnett concur, though with a different emphasis. 'At worst', they say, 'the current wave of apparatchiks seem to act as comfort blankets for ministers who have discarded their former idealism'.[29]

This leaves two significant sources of policy that are well attested, though virtually un-researched. One is the prime minister's 'senior' policy advisers. Thatcher appointed some prominent businessmen such as Sir Derek Rayner, a leading department store manager, and Sir Roy Griffiths, a leading supermarket manager, as special advisers to herself, and they were openly given more influence on policy than permanent civil servants. Blair followed suit, and under his personalized and highly-centralized system of government the influence of his senior policy advisers was very considerable – with sometimes disastrous results, since his choice of advisers was sometimes lamentable. This was notoriously true of Andrew Adonis, his senior policy adviser on education, elevated to the peerage as Lord Adonis after the 2005 election and put in charge of schools policy in London. Adonis was one of the most widely-despised figures of Blair's court, credited with having got a series of disastrous education policies adopted through having the ear of the prime minister. The message would come to the department of education that 'Tony's office' was keen on 'specialist schools' or 'city academies', policies which were the brainchildren of Adonis, a journalist who had once written a book about social class in schools and was keen on private education. (Ted Wragg, a widely respected authority on education, and a comic script-writer on the

REVOLVING DOORS

side, created a fictional character called 'Tony Zoffis' whose ignorant prejudices successive education ministers had to swallow).[30]

Another example, in the other main field of social policy, health care, is Simon Stevens, mentioned earlier. Before his appointment as Blair's senior health policy adviser he had been a middle-level hospital manager. He believed strongly in replacing the national health service with a market open to private providers, and this is what happened, in spite of the fact that this policy was never openly acknowledged, let alone put before the electorate in any of Labour's manifestos, and in spite of its disastrous long-term implications.

The other significant source of policy, and perhaps the most significant change in the operation of the state under the neoliberal policy regime, is the employment in key civil service posts of senior staff on secondment from the private sector. In 2004 the head of strategy in the Department of Health, for example, was on secondment from the management consultancy Pricewaterhouse Coopers, a leading advocate of the privatization of public services, and especially health care. In some departments the circulation of personnel between the civil service and the private sector has become commonplace, and the delay required before civil servants can take up lucrative private sector posts, in which they can put their inside knowledge of government at the service of companies, has also been progressively shortened. This so-called 'revolving door' between the state and the private sector has long been notorious in the field of defence, which accounts for a huge share of public spending.[31] Now it is becoming more general throughout the higher civil service.[32]

The chief focus of critics hitherto has tended to be on the conflicts of interest involved in this, especially the extent to which the prospect of lucrative private employment may influence the judgment of senior civil servants who should be guided solely by the public interest, and this is certainly a serious issue.[33] But the role played by private sector personnel seconded to policy-making roles in government today is more far-reaching. Faced with the demand to become business-like, and to pursue business-friendly policies, senior civil servants understandably reach out to business for help. What they get may not in fact be great expertise, but it always involves the importation of the general world-view inculcated in American business schools and disseminated through global management teams and financial markets. And with the collapse of the idea of a distinctively public domain goes the disappearance of any clear concept of the public interest as something different from and deeper than the collective interest of the corporations that dominate the economy. In effect, the corporate agenda is installed in the state; or to put it another way, public policy-making itself is 'outsourced'.

Entrepreneurialism and the use of evidence

Running through the history of the formation of the neoliberal policy regime is the emergence of a new ideal type, displacing that of the rational Weberian bureaucrat: the entrepreneur. What politicians admire, and want at the top of the state apparatus, are assertive, 'big' men (very rarely women), capable of some ruthlessness, strong on 'mission statements' and targets and impatient with detail, which they are apt to dismiss as the stock-in-trade of professional 'seers of difficulties' who will never accomplish anything. Civil servants have been seriously discouraged from playing their traditional role of screening out unworkable ideas. What is valued is a willingness to achieve whatever 'targets' the government decides it wants met, brushing aside obstacles and costs. The fact that so many 'can-do' businessmen of the kind politicians now hold up as models for senior civil servants to emulate – Gerald Ronson, Jim Slater, Jonathan Aitken, Robert Maxwell, Asil Nadir, John Gunn, Richard Brewster, David S. Smith, John Ashcroft – have eventually crashed spectacularly and/or gone to jail or been otherwise disgraced, losing (or in some cases stealing) the savings of thousands of people in the process, does not seem to dim their admiration.[34]

The result is a new attitude towards evidence. Evidence needed for policy-making relating to global market forces – statistical evidence on production, trade and finance, for example – is taken seriously. Evidence relating to socio-cultural adjustment policies is another matter (unless, of course, it is polling evidence on what voters are thinking and feeling, which is taken most seriously of all). Evidence that looks supportive of ideas to which the government is committed tends to be accepted uncritically. Contrary evidence tends to be dismissed. In Blair's entourage even pointing to the existence of contrary evidence comes to be treated as close to treason: 'critics of public-private partnerships, foundation hospitals and [university] tuition fees are branded not as participants in a reasonable debate about the direction of policy but relics of the party's dark ages, mad lefties jeopardizing the government's future'.[35] Outside Whitehall, consistently pointing to the existence of politically inconvenient evidence leads to professional marginalization or even – if the inconvenience is great enough – persecution. A cabal of obedient government backbenchers, for example, abused parliamentary privilege to make a scurrilous attack on the work of Professor Allyson Pollock, whose analyses of the private financing of hospital building had left that policy widely discredited.[36] Other examples of the persecution of critics, especially but not only by Blair's former spokesman Alastair Campbell, abound.[37]

That this should have become more or less normal, however, presupposes certain enabling conditions. Four stand out: the replacement of the culture of Royal Commissions by the culture of 'grey literature'; the loss of critical independence on the part of the academic research community; the de-politicisation of the electorate; and the return to respectability of irrational belief.

A lot of fun used to be had at the expense of Royal Commissions, seen as devices for indefinitely postponing action on controversial issues by appointing a group of the 'great and good' to mull them over inconsequentially for years. But Royal Commissions not only invited the best experts to give evidence, written and oral, but also commissioned research, and all of this was published in full, along with the Commissioners' final reports. Their recommendations could languish unimplemented, but the published research and evidence, publicly given and publicly interrogated, constituted a significant obstacle to the implementation of policies that flew in the face of the best evidence there was. Today, however, no one under the age of 45 has known the policy culture of which Royal Commissions were a significant part.

In place of the products of Royal Commissions there is 'grey literature'. Most definitions of grey literature focus on the idea that it is literature 'made available to the general public by public and private sector organizations whose function is not primarily publishing'.[38] As governments cut back on free access to even routine official statistics, and as privatization makes more and more public activity 'commercially confidential', grey literature has acquired a sort of respectability by default. Journals and conferences are devoted to it. What strikes the enquirer concerned with truth, however, is that organizations that are not primarily publishers lack a strong interest in the validity of what they nonetheless publish. Whereas a non-fiction or journal publisher, or a serious newspaper, has a reputation for truth to protect, many if not most other organizations are not necessarily concerned with this. As anyone who has tried to use grey literature soon discovers, data and judgments that have not been peer-reviewed or otherwise tested for accuracy and reliability cannot be relied on. But grey literature is increasingly cited in support of government policy.

The use of bad evidence is also less subject to informed criticism by the scientific community than would have been the case 25 years ago. The corruption of research in the natural sciences by corporate funding is a well-known problem, yet science research is more and more dependent on corporate money.[39] And by a different route, university-based social science in Britain has now also become increasingly oriented to market values and interests. Unlike US social science, British social science has always been predominantly state-funded. Under the liberal/social democratic policy regime the funding was distributed through research councils run by social scientists, with substantial independence from the government. Nor have British social scientists experienced the pressures to conform from right-wing vigilantes that have reinforced the prevailing political conformity of American social science.[40] British social scientists might be 'pro-market', but there was no obvious career incentive to be so.

Under Thatcher, however, this began to change. General government funding of universities was put on a market-oriented footing. Every degree course now had to be justified by a 'business plan' showing how the cost of the staff needed to teach it would be met out of the student income it would earn, and the research funding that the staff could be expected to secure. Eventually, 'under-studented' departments were downsized or closed. Government support for research through the universities' 'core funding' also declined (from 58.8 per cent of all research funding in 1984 to 35.1 per cent in 1997), and this support was now allocated on a selective basis. Under a periodic Research Assessment Exercise first introduced in 1986, departments with highly-ranked research output receive dramatically higher-than-average funding, while poorly-ranked departments receive dramatically less, or none at all. The share of research funding accounted for by work commissioned directly by either government departments or business rose from 15 per cent to 20.8 per cent of the total between 1984 and 1997, while the share coming from the government-funded research councils rose from 17.2 per cent to 24.1 per cent.[41]

In the case of the Economic and Social Research Council, reorganized under Thatcher in 1985, the bulk of its research funding was much more focussed than before on themes seen as relevant to the promotion of national economic competitiveness.[42] Individual researchers could still get smaller grants for critical work, but the attractions of landing serious money – grants of several million pounds over five years are not uncommon – for major centres and programmes of applied research were obvious, and a new generation of well-funded academics emerged, wielding considerable patronage among younger researchers willing to work within the neoliberal paradigm.

The combined effect of all these changes has been to make research within that paradigm well rewarded, and therefore highly valued by university administrators, while effective public criticism of government policies is to say the least not warmly encouraged. As a result the topics chosen for study, and the questions asked, have undergone a significant shift. The quantity of research has risen but its analytic and critical quality has declined. This may be no truer of political science than of other social science disciplines, but it is especially obvious in the study of politics. Roelofs' critique of American political science now largely fits its British counterpart. To take just one example:

> Political scientists... study parties and interest groups, yet the latters' creation and funding are usually neglected. The interlocking directorates among interest groups, foundations, and corporations are generally ignored. Professional associations, conferences of state officials, think tanks, and integrative organizations such as the Social Science Research Council and the American Council of Learned Societies are rarely examined in political science research. Thus indexes in American government textbooks sometimes list Ford, Betty, and omit the Ford Foundation.[43]

The same topics are also ignored, and the same questions are not asked, in Britain. Denham and Garnett, for example, the foremost academic experts on think tanks in Britain, make no effort to analyze the sources of their funding and the effect of this on what the tanks think about, and the conclusions they reach. There is a general de-politicisation of even political research.[44] Academic social scientists who offer informed public criticism of government policies have become an endangered species. It is more rewarding to engage in the kind of political punditry notably practised by Tony Giddens, a former director of the London School of Economics (LSE) and high priest of the Third Way ('somewhere between the Second Coming and the Fourth Dimension');[45] or John Gray, an LSE professor of European political theory, once a Thatcherite and now a convert to oriental mysticism and animal liberation.[46]

The fact that few social scientists are serious critics of public policy facilitates the de-politicisation of the electorate. Britain has not undergone – yet – an intellectual takeover of the kind successfully carried out by the far right in the US since the late 1960s, at the cost of hundreds of millions of dollars a year, via the creation or capture of right-wing think tanks, magazines, newspapers, publishers, television channels, radio stations and even whole universities.[47] But three quarters of British national newspaper circulation has long been owned and controlled by right-wing press barons, often North American, and the popular titles are prone to extreme bias, if not outright lies.[48] And concessions by successive governments of both major parties to corporate media interests have steadily enlarged the scope for private broadcasters and forced public service broadcasters to compete for increasingly fragmented audience shares.[49] News and current affairs have been steadily cut back in favour of entertainment. The bizarrely mis-named 'reality TV' shows that dominated the schedules in the early 2000s were a sign of the times. The critical context for serious policy debate has been significantly eroded.

And then there is the general revival of irrational belief, entertainingly reviewed by Francis Wheen in *How Mumbo-Jumbo Conquered the World*. The publicly-owned and public-service television channel, Channel 4, for example, ran a programme on nutrition hosted by a 'clinical nutritionist', complete with white coat, and continued it even when her credentials were exposed as worthless (the *Guardian*'s 'bad science' watchdog was able to buy her professional certificate for $60 for his deceased cat).[50] And the government's infatuation with business and businessmen meant that the cliché-ridden and unsubstantiated outpourings of business gurus would be taken seriously by the architects of public service 'reforms'. All this is bad enough. But what about 'alternative' medicine, advocated by the heir to the throne and adopted, partly as a sop to populism, by some parts of the National Health Service? Wheen's bracing comment that "'complementary" and "alternative" are essentially euphemisms for "dud"' would no doubt be dismissed by New Labour's boot-boys as 'elitist'.[51]

Blair's deference towards mumbo-jumbo was usually attributed to the influence of his wife. Authors sympathetic to Cherie Blair, however, say that he shared her flakier interests.[52] If so, it helps to explain his refusal to condemn the teaching of creationism in a state secondary school in Gateshead that was captured by creationists. 'A more diverse school system', he said, 'will deliver better results for our children'.[53] The Blairs' spiritual tastes were perhaps more in tune with the zeitgeist than the scepticism of their critics, but it was not without consequences for public policy. Just as Thatcher had openly sympathized with the Ayatollah who called for Salman Rushdie to be murdered for writing *The Satanic Verses*, Blair's home affairs minister refused to condemn the violence by Sikh fundamentalists in Birmingham in late 2004 that succeeded in closing a play they found offensive, saying that 'both the theatre and the protesters had a right to free speech'.[54] On the contrary the government proposed to introduce legislation to make it a crime to 'incite to religious hatred'. (No law was proposed to criminalize the suppression by pharmaceutical companies of evidence showing that a profitable drug was dangerous, or the invention of evidence to win parliamentary assent to start a war.)

The influence of all these factors means that there is remarkably little adverse comment on the steep decline that has occurred since 1980 in the quality of government policy documents, whose level of argumentation and use of evidence is all too often inversely related to the quality of their presentation (in the style of corporate reports, complete with executive summaries and flashy graphics). They are designed to look principled, purposeful and rational. In reality what they constantly reveal is the subordination of policy to what are seen as market imperatives, presented as some sort of balance between principle and pragmatism, tradition and innovation. Stefan Collini's dissection of the Labour government's 2003 white paper on *The Future of Higher Education* could be replicated for a distressingly high proportion of them. He begins with a quotation from the white paper's introduction:

> We see a higher education sector which meets the needs of the economy in terms of trained people, research and technology transfer. At the same time it needs to enable all suitably qualified individuals to develop their potential both intellectually and personally, and to provide the necessary storehouse of expertise in science and technology, and the arts and humanities which defines our civilization and culture.

'It is hardly surprising', Collini comments,

> that universities in Britain are demoralized. Even those statements which are clearly intended to be upbeat affirmations of their importance have a way of making you feel slightly ill. It is not simply the fact that no single institution could successfully achieve all the aims crammed into this unlovely paragraph... It is also the thought of that room in Whitehall where these collages are assembled. As the findings from the latest survey of focus groups come in, an official cuts out all those things which earned a positive rating and glues them together in a straight line. When a respectable number have been accumulated in this way, s/he puts a dot at the end and calls it a sentence.

> There are two sentences in that paragraph. The first, which is clear enough though not a thing of beauty, says that the main aim of universities is to turn out people and ideas capable of making money. The second, which is neither clear nor beautiful, says there are a lot of other points that it's traditional to mention in this connection, and that they're all good things too, in their way, and that the official with the glue-pot has been having a busy day, and that we've lost track of the subject of the verb in the last line, and that it may be time for another full stop.[55]

The unresolved conflict – at the level of discourse, that is – between market and non-market objectives, the interpenetration of electoral aims and public interest concerns, the loss of respect for (or even serious interest in) research and evidence, the waning of analytic skills and the apotheosis of the entrepreneur – combine to produce defective reasoning and exaggerated promises. Careful argument and the adducing of evidence give way to 'values', 'mission statements' and 'targets'.[56]

In the USA, the imperial heartland, indifference to evidence has been given an explicit imperial rationale. In 2002 Ron Suskind was told by one of Bush's 'senior advisers' that

> guys like me were 'in what we call the reality-based community', which he defined as people 'who believe that solutions emerge from your judicious study of discernible reality... That's not the way the world really works anymore', he continued. 'We're an empire now, and when we act, we create our own reality... We're history's actors... and you, all of you, will be left to just study what we do'.[57]

This kind of lumpen-Hegelian rhetoric is perhaps a step too far for most apparatchiks of a sub-imperial power like Britain.[58] But it is the principle on which a great deal of policy is based.

Conclusion: the dependency of our time

Nothing described here is likely to be unfamiliar to anyone in the smaller countries of the 'South', where national policy has almost always been largely driven by external market forces, backed by foreign political and military power. One could say that 'dependency' now affects all countries except the USA. Of course there are big differences of degree, but the policy regime of even a major post-industrial state like Britain is no longer as radically different from that of a 'banana republic' as most people in Britain imagine. The installation of management consultants in key government policy-making posts is not entirely unlike the installation of officers from the World Bank in the ministries of an African state. Structural adjustment is in progress in both.

Thanks to Thatcher and Blair, Britain has advanced farther and more willingly along this path than other west European countries, and since cultural change lags behind material change the gap between reality and official rhetoric may be larger than elsewhere.

Perhaps inherited ideas and illusions about sovereignty, democracy and the public interest confront the new reality of global market forces and corporate power more starkly than in other comparable countries.[59] But all countries must now travel more or less the same path, for the same reason: policy-making must always try to conceal the basic fact that economic and social policy now has to be made on capital's terms. This is not something voters like to be told, and the policies capital demands are often electorally unpalatable. As far as possible, therefore, these policies are increasingly made in secret and their likely effects concealed.

The dismantling of the higher civil service inherited from the late nineteenth century corresponds to the substitution of the rationality of the market for the instrumental rationality of a bureaucracy. A preference for entrepreneurs – whether actual businessmen seconded in from the private sector, or civil servants with entrepreneurial personalities and outlooks – focused on 'getting things done', and an impatience with bureaucrats professionally concerned with the wider implications of policy ('ensuring all points of view are considered' with, no doubt, a sometimes irritating touch of *noblesse oblige*), makes sense in these terms.[60] The state becomes not just more and more responsive to capital, but more and more closely integrated with it. And the risks involved are not borne by the new entrepreneurs of the state – any more than they are in today's corporate world – but by the public.

Endnotes

1 Blair's statement to parliament no doubt relied on what his senior officials told him, so he may have told untruths unwittingly: but one of the noteworthy aspects of the whole affair was the way the responsibility that is supposed to be shouldered by ministers, and not least the prime minister, was constantly shuffled off onto officials – who also remained unpunished.

2   'Sexed up' was the expression allegedly used by David Kelly, the source for Gilligan's story. The expression preferred by the prime minister's office and Scarlett was 'presentational changes'.

3   'Never Mind the Truth', *Guardian*, 21 March 2005.

4   Richard G.A. Feachem, N.K Sekhri and K.L. White, 'Getting More For Their Dollar: A Comparison of the NHS with California's Kaiser Permanente', *BMJ*, 324, 2002, pp. 135-43. For the critiques see 'Rapid Responses' on the *BMJ*'s website, www.bmj.com, a selection of which was later printed in the *BMJ*, Vol. 324, 2002, pp. 1332-35.

5   The Kaiser article's authors declined to respond to the criticisms, and the BMJ declined to print a systematic critique. The reason for the latter decision remains obscure; it seemed to reflect the growing tendency of the medical establishment to make its peace with the government's determination to impose a market system on the National Health Service.

6   *Guardian*, 4 February 2005. 'Czar' was the popular name for a series of appointments of individuals to oversee the achievement of government targets in primary care, cancer care, drug abuse, etc.

7   The quoted expressions are from the famous Northcote-Trevelyan report adopted by Gladstone as prime minister and finally imposed throughout the civil service by the end of the nineteenth century.

8   David Marquand, *Decline of the Public: The Hollowing out of Citizenship* (Cambridge: Polity Press, 2004), pp. 53-54.

9   Thomas Balogh, 'The Apotheosis of the Dilettante', in Hugh Thomas, ed., *The Establishment* (London: Anthony Blond, 1959).

10 Quoted in Andrew Gamble, *Britain in Decline*, fourth edition (London: Macmillan, 1994), p. 99.

11 'The Origins of the Administrative Elite', *New Left Review*, 162, 1987, p. 34.

12 This section draws on chapter 3 of my *Market Driven Politics: Neoliberal Democracy and the Public Interest* (London: Verso, 2000).

13 See Leo Panitch and Colin Leys, *The End of Parliamentary Socialism*, Second Edition (London: Verso, 2001), chapters 10 and 13.

14 Jim Prior, *A Balance of Power*, quoted in Peter Hennessy, *Whitehall* (London: Fontana, 1990), pp. 633-34.

15 Marquand, *Decline*, pp. 109-10. For a frankly embarrassing example of grovel see the speech given on September 10, 2003, by Sir John Bourn, the Comptroller and Auditor General, to the PPP [Public Private Partnerships] Forum, which represents the new industrial sector conjured into being by the private financing of public services. Bourn was nominally employed by parliament to check public spending, but he sounded exactly like someone hoping for a job with one of the companies involved.

16 Hennessey, *Whitehall*, p. 633, quoting an unnamed senior civil servant.

17 *Guardian*, 24 March 2004.

18 *Guardian*, 3 February 2005.

19 The government adopted the minority report of the two pro-market members of the Sutherland Commission on Care of the Aged, appointed in 1997, and balked completely at dealing with the compromise recommendations of the Wakeham Commission on the reform of the House of Lords, appointed in 1999.

20 Forty-seven significant departmental enquiries were appointed in the 1970s, 24 in the 1980s, and 13 in the 1990s (David Butler and Gareth Butler, *Twentieth-Century British Political Facts* (Basingstoke: Macmillan, 2000).

21 In the mid-1990s the Rand Corporation had 950 staff and a budget of $50-100 million, and four others had budgets of more than $10 million. The biggest British think tank, the Policy Studies Institute, with 54 staff and an annual income of $6.5 million in the late 1990s, was half as big as the fifth largest US think tank, the Heritage Foundation (see Andrew Denham and Mark Garnett, *British Think Tanks and the Climate of Opinion*, London: University College London Press 1988, p. 5).

22 Ibid., p. 244.

23 Ibid.

24 'Think Tanks? No Thanks', *Guardian*, 18 July 2002. Birt was a former Director General of the BBC brought into the prime minister's office to do 'blue skies thinking' – initially, apparently, about transport, a field in which he had no expertise at all.

25 Richard Cockett, *Thinking the Unthinkable: Think Tanks and the Economic Counter-Revolution, 1931-1983* (London: HarperCollins,

1995). See also Radhika Desai, 'Second-Hand Dealers in Ideas: Think Tanks and Thatcherite Hegemony', *New Left Review*, I/203, 1994.

26 Bennett, 'Think Tanks?'.

27 See Stephen Court, 'Think or Sink', *Public Finance*, 11 October 2002.

28 *1 Out of 10* (London: Vintage, 2005), p. 71.

29 Denham and Garnett, 'A "Hollowed Out" Tradition? British Think Tanks in the Twenty-First Century', in Diane Stone and Mark Garnett, eds., *Think Tank Traditions: Policy Research and the Politics of Ideas* (Manchester: Manchester University Press, 2004), pp. 232-46.

30 On Adonis' appointment as an unelected minister Francis Beckett catalogued the long series of disastrous educational policies for which he had been personally responsible: see 'The Rise of Tony Zoffis', *Guardian*, 11 May 2005.

31 This has been documented for the post-Cold War years by the UK Campaign Against Arms Trade, in *Who Calls the Shots? How Government-Corporate Collusion Drives Arms Exports* (London: February, 2005).

32 Peter Oborne thinks the critical turning point in the erosion of the boundary between the state and the private sector came with the appointment of Sir Andrew Turnbull as Cabinet Secretary in 2002. According to him, Turnbull's predecessor had fought hard to get a Civil Service Act passed, which would demarcate the boundary. 'One of Turnbull's first acts as Cabinet Secretary was to make it known that he did not believe that the Civil Service Act, and thus the protections it would have entrenched, were necessary'. *The Rise of Political Lying* (London: The Free Press, 2005), p. 189.

33 For examples of the effects of this see Allyson Pollock, *NHS plc: The Privatization of our Healthcare* (London: Verso, 2004), pp. 4-9.

34 This list is from Francis Wheen, *How Mumbo-Jumbo Conquered the World* (London: Harper Perennial, 2004), pp. 59-62, and refers only to fallen business idols in Britain. A list of fallen business idols in the US, such as Enron's Kenneth Lay, Jeff Skilling and Andrew Fastow, or WorldCom's Bernie Ebbers, would be a lot longer.

35 Anne Perkins, 'Regime Change or Climate Change, Tony?', *New Statesman*, 29 September 2003. Foundation hospitals – freeing the country's publicly owned hospitals from central government control

and making them compete (or collaborate) with private ones – were the prelude to introducing a health care market. Introducing so-called 'top-up' fees for university students was another market-driven idea, deeply unpopular within the governing party.

36 For Pollock's account of this affair see *NHS plc*, pp. 209-13.

37 See Peter Oborne and Simon Walters, *Alastair Campbell* (London: Aurum Press, 2004).

38 Michael Quinion, 'Grey Literature' in World Wide Words, at http://www.worldwidewords.org.

39 For a discussion of the capture of British university scientific research by corporations see George Monbiot, *Captive State* (Basingstoke: Macmillan 2000), chapter 9.

40 Examples have recurred throughout the history of American social science, and not just in the McCarthy era. Two recent cases seem to be the result of efforts by pro-Israeli organizations to get rid of professors seen as pro-Palestinian: Joseph Massad at Columbia University, and Tariq Ramadan, a Swiss professor denied a visa to teach at Notre Dame. The case of the anthropologist David Graeber, 'let go' from Yale in 2005 on political grounds, is more typical.

41 Ted Tapper and Brian Salter, 'The Politics of Governance in Higher Education: The Case of the Research Assessment Exercise', *OxCHEPS Occasional Paper No. 6*, Oxford Centre for Higher Education Policy Studies, Oxford, May 2002, p. 29. The authors comment that 'in the age of global capital… the market is becoming an increasingly significant player and the universities… will have to determine what structures of governance they need to control its input' (p. 30). Their own view, however, is that all further developments in the research role of the universities will be determined by the government.

42 In 2001-2002 the Council had seven priority themes for centres and programmes in receipt of major funding, accounting for 63 per cent of its funding for specific research projects. They were: economic performance and development; social stability and exclusion; work and organization; knowledge, communication and learning; governance and citizenship; environment and human behaviour (*Economic and Social Research Council Annual Report 2001-2002*).

43 Joan Roelofs, *Foundations and Public Policy* (Albany, NY: State University of New York Press, 2003), p. 32.

44 Some American graduate students were recently invited to consider this question. They were highly intrigued. This, they said, was the sort of thing you get excited about when you are not 'doing political science'. In their own work they were using an 'actor-oriented stakeholder analysis', and were very much on their guard against 'left conspiracy theories'.

45 Wheen, *Mumbo-Jumbo*, pp. 224-25.

46 Before he was a Thatcherite Gray was a socialist, and between being a Thatcherite and an animal liberationist he was a traditional conservative. His home page announced that he is available for long-term consultancies.

47 For a brilliant summary of this see Lewis Lapham, 'Tentacles of Rage: The Republican Propaganda Mill, A Brief History', in *Harper's Magazine*, September 2004, pp. 31-41.

48 The crude fabrications of the British tabloid press are periodically recorded by Roy Greenslade in the *Guardian*'s weekly Media supplement.

49 See Leys, *Market Driven Politics*, chapter 5.

50 'You don't need to be human; you don't even have to be alive. No exam, no check-up on your qualifications and no assessment of your practice' (Ben Goldacre, reporting how his dead cat Henrietta became a certified member of the American Association of Nutritional Consultants, in *Guardian Life*, 19 August 2004).

51 Nick Cohen, *Pretty Straight Guys* (London: Faber and Faber, 2003), p. 28: 'Sceptics were elitist because they refused to share the people's authentic elation at the election of Tony Blair or grief at the death of Princess Di. Critics of business were elitist because they presumed to know better than hundreds of millions of consumers... The knowledgeable on any subject... were elitist because they knew more than the ignorant...'.

52 Francis Beckett and David Hencke, *The Blairs and Their Court* (London: Aurum Press, 2004), pp. 278-9.

53 Parliamentary response to Jenny Tonge MP, quoted in Wheen, *Mumbo-Jumbo*, p. 114.

54 Lee Glendinning, *Guardian*, 27 December 2004. The personal views of the minister in question, Fiona MacTaggart, are not known. Her comments sounded like a craven capitulation to violence – and the

threats made to the playwright, herself a Sikh, and her family – in an effort to retain the Sikh vote.

55 'HiEdBiz', *London Review of Books*, 25(21), 6 November 2003.

56 The unfortunate British Prisons Service, hived off by the Conservatives as an 'executive agency', free – in theory – from day to day control by the Home Office, rejoiced in having 'one Statement of Purpose, one Vision, five Values, six Goals, seven Strategic Priorities and eight Key Performance Indicators' (Wheen, *Mumbo-Jumbo*, pp. 56-57).

57 'Without a Doubt', *New York Times*, 17 October 2004.

58 But Blair's right hand man Peter Mandelson is quoted as saying: 'our job is to create the truth' (Oborne, *The Rise of Political Lying*, p. 3).

59 A conjunctural factor of some importance in the British case was the determination of Blair, Brown and Mandelson to 'outspin' the right-wing media that had trashed the efforts of the party's former leader, Neil Kinnock, to return Labour to power in 1992. Although Oborne (in *The Rise of Political Lying*) is hostile witness, it is hard to dispute his judgment that what began as an understandable reaction to victimization ended up as 'the useful lies of the ruling class'.

60 Barbara Harriss-White suggests that 'perhaps the new entrepreneurialism is a transfer to the state of a social institution developed for the quite different "factor endowments" of the firm, where entrepreneurial behaviour is rewarded with monopoly rents; or is it perhaps a mask used cynically by both capital and the state because the 'rent' is the consolidation of a totalizing system?' (personal communication).

Printed in the United Kingdom
by Lightning Source UK Ltd.
128058UK00001B/141/P